GOLDEN ARROW

"Rejoice, My Daughter, because the hour approaches when the most beautiful work under the sun will be born."
—Our Lord
To Sister Mary of St. Peter

(Our Lord refers here to the work of reparation to the Holy Face, which He revealed is destined to be the means of defeating atheistic Communism and restoring peace to the world.)

SISTER MARY OF ST. PETER
AND OF THE HOLY FAMILY
1816-1848
Carmelite Nun of Tours, France
To Whom Our Lord imparted His revelations
About Devotion to the Holy Face of Jesus

THE
GOLDEN ARROW

THE AUTOBIOGRAPHY AND REVELATIONS
OF SISTER MARY OF ST. PETER
(1816–1848)
ON DEVOTION TO
THE HOLY FACE OF JESUS

Edited by
Dorothy Scallan

Translated by
Fr. Emeric B. Scallan, S.T.B.

Based upon and quoting authentic French manucripts
emanating directly from the archives
of the Monastery of Discalced Carmelites, at Tours, France,
where Sister Mary of St. Peter lived and died.

"By My Holy Face you will work
wonders."
—Our Lord
To Sister Mary of St. Peter

TAN Books
An Imprint of Saint Benedict Press, LLC
Charlotte, North Carolina

Nihil Obstat: John M. A. Fearns, S.T.D.
                    Censor Librorum

Imprimatur: ✠ Francis Cardinal Spellman
                    Archbishop of New York
                    March 15, 1954

The *Nihil Obstat* and *Imprimatur* are official declarations that a book or pamphlet is free of doctrinal or moral error. No implication is contained therein that those who have granted the *Nihil Obstat* and *Imprimatur* agree with the contents, opinions or statements expressed.

This book was originally published in hardbound in 1954 by The William Frederick Press, New York, New York. It was reissued by that company in a paperbound edition in 1973 under the title, *Veronica's Veil*, giving the editor's name as Doris Sheridan (pen name of Dorothy Scallan, the sister of Fr. Emeric Scallan). This present (third) edition is photographically reproduced complete and unabridged from the first edition, with the new elements of the second edition added, and using once again the original title.

Library of Congress Catalog Card No.: 90-70258

ISBN: 978-0-89555-389-8

Printed and bound in the United States of America.

TAN Books
An Imprint of Saint Benedict, LLC
Charlotte, North Carolina
2012

THIS VOLUME IS DEDICATED

IN THIS MARIAN YEAR OF GRACE

TO

MARY IMMACULATE, THE MOTHER OF GOD,

THAT SHE MAY OBTAIN FOR US THE TRIUMPH OF

THE WORK OF REPARATION

THROUGH

THE HOLY FACE OF HER DIVINE SON

WE HEREBY declare that we absolutely and entirely conform to the decree of Urban VIII with respect to the terms of eulogy or veneration applied to the servants of God, Sister Mary of St. Peter, and others, as well as to the Divine revelations mentioned in the present book; and, moreover, that we by no means anticipate the decisions of the Holy See.

THE "GOLDEN ARROW" PRAYER

MAY the most holy, most sacred, most
adorable, most incomprehensible and
unutterable Name of God be always praised,
blessed, loved, adored and glorified, in
Heaven, on earth, and under the earth, by all
the creatures of God, and by the Sacred Heart
of Our Lord Jesus Christ in the Most Holy
Sacrament of the Altar. Amen.

After receiving this prayer, Sister Mary of St. Peter was given a vision
in which she saw the Sacred Heart of Jesus delightfully wounded by this
"Golden Arrow," as torrents of graces streamed from It for the conversion of sinners.

ACKNOWLEDGMENTS

I WISH to express my gratitude to the Discalced Carmelite Nuns, at Tours, France, for presenting me with authoritative manuscripts in the French language, used exclusively in the preparation of this English version of the Autobiography and the Revelations of Sister Mary of St. Peter and of the Holy Family, a professed religious of their own community, who died in the odor of sanctity on July 8, 1848.

Furthermore, I here express my warm thanks to the Priests at the Oratory of the Holy Face, at Tours, France, for their encouragement and permission to translate the French documents on the Work of Reparation, emanating from the Seat of the Archconfraternity of the Holy Face, at Tours.

Finally, I take this occasion to acknowledge with gratitude the literary and spiritual assistance rendered me in the preparation of this book by Miss Doris Sheridan.* Her noteworthy research on the Cult of the Holy Face has been evidenced by her extensive writings on this topic, and particularly climaxed by her most recent book, *The Whole World Will Love Me* (1954, The William-Frederick Press, New York), which strikingly bears out that it was the Little Flower's devotion to the Holy Face which drove her to her unparalleled heights of sanctity.

EMERIC B. SCALLAN, S.T.B.

---

*Pen name of Dorothy Scallan.—*Editor,* 1990.

PUBLISHER'S PREFACE

(Adapted for the 1990 edition from the Second Edition of the book)

FATHER EMERIC B. SCALLAN pursued his studies for the priesthood at St. Mary's Seminary, Baltimore, and in Rome, where he was ordained. The late Bishop Cornelius Van de Ven of New Orleans appointed Father Scallan as the first editor of the New Orleans diocesan newspaper and thereby launched him on a career in Catholic publishing.

After spending a number of years in the press, Father Scallan noted the alarming spread of atheism. He became convinced that of all the published Catholic material that came to his attention as editor, the Revelations of the French cloistered Carmelite Nun, Sister Mary of St. Peter, dealt directly with the problem of overcoming atheism and restoring peace to the world. He therefore translated her autobiography and helped his sister Dorothy with two other books dealing with this single theme, namely, that of offering the bruised Holy Face of Jesus to the Eternal Father in reparation for blasphemy.

At present, during these post-conciliar years, irreligion and other direct affronts against the Church have multiplied to drastic proportions. Not only in secular spheres, but even in quarters called "Catholic" there is a sort of infamous jabbing at all things Catholic, and that on a wide, public scale, which actually derogates from the extrinsic honor due the Holy Name of God. For this reason, and also because recently there have been repeated requests for the book treating the Revelations on the Holy Face—from both religious and the laity—a new, third edition has been undertaken. This current book, in flexible cover, is an unabridged edition of the first edition of *The Golden Arrow.*

Besides this book, there are two more volumes, forming together a sort of "trilogy" on the Holy Face Devotion for our times. *The Holy Man of Tours* (formerly titled *God Demands Reparation*), by Dorothy Scallan, deals with the life of a French attorney, Leo Dupont, who was personally acquainted with Sister Mary of St. Peter, to whom the revelations of this book were imparted by Our Lord. After her death, he became an apostle, spreading the cult of the Holy Face, not only in France, but to the most distant points of the world. After Sr. Mary's death and before official Church approval of the Holy Face Devotion, Leo Dupont developed great personal devotion to the Holy Face of Jesus (inspired by the revelations of Sr. Mary), to which he was so committed that for some 30 years he kept a perpetual lamp burning before a true replica of Veronica's Veil in a place of honor and veneration in the drawing room of his home in Tours, France. Before long, he was working miracles by applying the oil of this lamp to people's diseased or injured members. In time, his success and fame as a miracle-worker became so astounding that Pope Pius IX (1846-1878) declared him to be perhaps the greatest thaumaturgist (miracle-worker) in Church history. The cause for his beatification is in process.

The third book in this series is entitled *The Whole World Will Love Me*, by Dorothy Scallan, and is a biography of St. Therese of the Child Jesus and of the Holy Face. In this definitive study, St. Therese is portrayed in her essential role as an adorer of the Holy Face, which practice sent her to such heights of sanctity that she has come to be esteemed as the greatest saint of modern times.

Father Scallan is one of five religious vocations in his family, two of whom became priests, two nuns, and one a brother in a religious order.

THE
GOLDEN ARROW

"Just as in an earthly kingdom money which is stamped with the picture of the sovereign or ruling executive of the country procures whatever one desires to purchase, so likewise in the Kingdom of Heaven, you shall obtain all that you desire by offering the coin of My precious Humanity which is My adorable Face."

—Our Lord
To Sr. Mary of St. Peter

The Holy Face of Jesus from the image on Veronica's veil.
(The veil is kept in St. Peter's Basilica, Rome.)

PART I

AUTOBIOGRAPHY
OF
SISTER MARY OF ST. PETER
AND OF THE HOLY FAMILY

1

SINCE YOU, Reverend Mother, think that it will redound to the glory of God and my own abasement that I should at this time write in all simplicity a brief account of my life, I will do so. While I have always had an aversion for writing about myself, I shall obey you, Reverend Mother, and perform this act with the aid of the Divine Infant Jesus. Remembering how forcibly grace has always assisted me whenever I was compelled by obedience to give you in writing a full report of the various communications which, in spite of my unworthiness, I have from time to time received from our Saviour regarding the Work of Reparation, I now place my pen in the hands of the Divine Child Jesus, imploring Him to write for me.

Thus shall God, the Father, be glorified by this short story of my life, because it will prove how by His power, He has brought forth from the barren soil of my soul, filled with flaws, imperfections and sins, such beautiful fruits for the glory of His Holy Name.

I was born October 4, 1816. This date is notable as the anniversary of the death of our holy mother, Saint Teresa, and it is also the feast of Saint Francis of Assisi, whose name my mother bore. I was baptized in the Church of St. Germain, in the city of Rennes, and given the names of Perrine Frances.

My poor mother received a sad gift, indeed, on that anniversary of her feast-day, in the birth of the little girl whose sicknesses and waywardness were to cause her so much worry.

Since my mother was of delicate health, she had to entrust

me, soon after I was born, to the care of a wet nurse, who was an excellent person. Then when I was but one month old, I met with an accident which could have caused my death, had it not been for God's special protection.

This good woman, my nurse, having gone out awhile, had left me in my cradle. One of her own small children picked me up and undoubtedly wishing to keep me warm brought me close to the fireplace. I fell out of the child's arms into the fire, and my face has ever since retained a mark from that burn. When my poor mother learned of this, she was very much distressed, and immediately took me away from that person's care.

I shall at this point relate one of my first traits of meanness. When I grew older, someone had told me about the accident. One day when this poor woman, my nurse, came to visit me, I received her very coldly, saying to her: "So, you have already burned one of my cheeks and do you come here today to scorch the other?"

When I was four years old I had an attack of scarlet fever which brought me close to death. My parents told me that I was in grave danger for nineteen days, during which time I could take no food except a small glass of cider. It always amused my father who used to laugh as he would recall to me that a beverage so poorly suited to my condition should have sustained me and preserved my life.

As soon as my reason began to develop, my parents, who were truly good and pious, taught me the first rudiments of Christian doctrine. However, I gave little evidence of a good disposition. I was easily moved to anger, and also had stubborn traits. My mother, being very devout, often took me with her to church, but in my restlessness I used to keep turning my head constantly to see everything that went on. Upon returning home from services, my mother never failed to punish me sternly for misbehaving in church.

Then too, I used to be so jealous of my sister, that they were obliged to separate us for some time. With all these faults, which made me very disagreeable, I was also proud and full of self-love. To make me realize and correct my many faults, my mother once said in front of me to my father: "Ah, this little girl is surely not our own. I think that she must have been exchanged in the nursery, for it is not possible that a child of ours could be as bad as this little one." That conversation did not please me in the least, and, in fact, I could not quite make up my mind how to take it.

When I was six and a half years old, I was taken to confession to accuse myself of all my faults.

Finally, however, I managed to win a victory over my pride. It happened that a poor, blind beggar used to pass in front of our house almost every day. He was very poorly dressed and often needed a charitable hand to guide him across the street. My parents had several times suggested to me that I offer the blind man my services, but the very thought seemed repugnant to me. Finally, one day doing great violence to myself, I took the poor blind man by the arm, and led him in the right direction. When I returned home it seemed to me that I had, indeed, performed a most heroic deed. After that whenever I was bad and my parents punished me, I forced myself not to resent their corrections, realizing that they were of great benefit to me. I began to feel grace reproaching me for my bad conduct.

About this time, in order to instill into me devotion to the Blessed Virgin, my parents would tell me of instances when this good Mother showered her protection on those who invoked her. Touched by these accounts of Mary's great power, I prayed to her to help me also, and I began to improve and soon became better. I now also began to like prayer, and no longer did I find it difficult to conduct myself properly in church. Returning home from High Mass on Sundays there were no more penances for me to perform as in the past. Now all this change for the good happened because I had begun to reason things out, and became wise, so that when something clashed with my wishes, I would think it over, and doing violence to myself I would say: "My God, I offer you this to atone for my sins."

My parents also had me attend the Catechism class which was held for the children of the parish. As I liked the instructions very much, I followed them attentively. I began now to be so well-behaved that compliments soon replaced the reproaches which I had been accustomed to receive. One day a lady said to my mother in front of me: "Madam, your little girl behaves in church like a person forty years old." But I believe that these compliments used to feed my self-love and so I began to make the Stations of the Cross. As I would read about the sufferings of our Saviour, my soul was deeply moved for I understood that my sins had caused them. Grieving, I would say to our Lord, "Oh, my Saviour, have you at least seen during your passion that one day I would be converted and would become all yours?" As I used to kiss the floor at each station, I invariably returned home with dust on my face. Our Lord allowed that this act of piety should result in a slight humiliation for me, for when my sister would get angry at me, she would call me "dirty nose." My virtue being yet very weak, I resented her sarcasm, and endured it as a very great trial.

Divine grace at this time attracted me strongly to God but I was not constant in doing good. I would fall and rise. Then having heard, though I do not remember from what source, that there was a kind of prayer called "mental" prayer, which was described as being more pleasing to God and more efficacious than "vocal" prayer, I strongly desired to practice it. I therefore said to myself: "I know what I will do. When I pray I will not pronounce the words and that will make it 'mental' prayer." But alas, when I had finished my prayers in this way, I became worried at not having said my morning and evening prayers.

Our Lord, seeing my desire, inspired me to think of His sufferings and of my sins. As I did so, I found myself weeping bitterly. Then somewhat later, our Lord permitted that I should be present at a sermon which treated entirely the subject of meditation. I, therefore, opened my ears and my heart to such a happy instruction, rejoicing to know at last how to make mental prayer.

Having reached the age of ten and one-half years, I prepared myself for my First Holy Communion by making a general confession. Through the mercy of God my heart was truly touched by His grace, and I received our divine Saviour with great fervor. Realizing how greatly I offended Him in my childhood, I now gave myself entirely to Him. That same day I received also the Sacrament of Confirmation, and was invested with the Scapular of Our Lady of Mount Carmel, which placed me under the protection of that tender Mother to whom I felt I owed my conversion. My confessor, seeing that I was entirely changed, gave me permission to receive Communion during the course of the year. This priest began also to marvel at the change which Divine Grace was working in my soul, and he on several occasions openly spoke to me on this subject. But invariably after saying a great deal that was complimentary to me and therefore pleasant to my ears, he never failed to humble me. Since I did not possess much humility, I would have preferred not receiving any of his praises at all, if they were meant to be followed by humiliations.

Our Divine Saviour, who kept watch on me, wished to purify my soul by interior sufferings and therefore sent me a severe trial, truly calculated to drive pride forever from my heart. Satan, seeing that his prey had escaped him, made some fierce attacks against my soul, but seeing himself turned out of his house, he went, undoubtedly, to seek, as it is said in the Gospel, seven spirits more wicked than himself, to attempt to force his way. I was, therefore, attacked by a thousand temptations, while my soul was steeped in darkness. I was ravaged with doubts and scruples. I believed myself committing sins every moment. I lost hold of myself. If I listened to a sermon, the devil would whisper curses and blasphemies into my ears. Evil thoughts tortured my mind. I was then only twelve years old but the sins of my past life would agonize my spirit. It would seem to me that I had not in the past confessed my sins well, and yet to confess them now appeared almost impossible because I would lose myself in endless examinations of conscience, and never felt myself well enough prepared when my turn came to enter the confessional.

Therefore, I would leave the church with my soul tortured with pain. As for praying, I could no longer find in it any consolation. I believed that all my prayers were bad and I would for that reason repeatedly start them over again. This repetition was as ridiculous as it was sad. My confessor did all he could to reassure me and to console me. But being so young and not having any experience with this sort of temptation, I found it difficult to explain to my director the full extent of the misery I endured. God was thus purifying my soul, for indeed during this time of trial I was very far from tasting the sweets of self-love.

Our Lord also tried me now with another cross in taking to Himself my dear mother whom I loved very much. I remembered having once heard that like myself, St. Teresa of Avila was only twelve years old also when she lost her mother. Following her example, I begged the Most Blessed Virgin to be my mother, and thus to replace her who died. The most holy Virgin must have granted my petition, for ever since that time I have always felt her maternal protection.

I continued to attend the advanced Catechism class for several years and used to receive Communion together with the other children. The priest who gave the religious instructions was very learned, and he is at present a bishop [in America]. I think he understood the sad state of my soul but since I never went to confession to him he was unable to offer me any consolation. However, it was he who preached the sermon that taught me how to make mental prayer, and later he did me much good.

But now to return to the topic of the Catechism class. When our special Feast-Day was approaching, the priest chose three girls to present in dialogue form a public debate. I was one of the three chosen and each of us had a part to learn. In this play my two companions had the role of recommending to me all the pleasures of this world, which they praised very highly. As for me, my role was to expose and show the emptiness and vanity of mere worldly pleasures. When the public discourse ended, one of my companions came to me saying that I had, no doubt, made a vow of poverty and that I would perhaps become a Carmelite nun. Thanks be to the Lord, I, indeed, later received the grace of that vocation. My two companions remained in the world and were married.

About this time it pleased God, at last, to deliver me from my interior darkness and my scruples. This happened when a charitable lady who had the same confessor that I had, knowing about my spiritual trial, had the kindness to speak to him about me. She evidently told him that I would leave church every time it was my turn to enter the confessional and so one day when my turn came round to enter immediately following behind her, as usual, suddenly deeming my preparation insufficient, I began to turn away. But to my surprise, the priest opening wide his confessional door beckoned me to enter, making me understand that he was ordering me to come and begin my confession without further delay. I excused myself saying that I had not yet finished my examination of conscience and that I had no contrition, but he paid no attention to my objections. I therefore submitted obediently and received absolution. "My daughter," the priest then said to me, "rest assured that this confession is one of the best of your whole life."

He then expressly forbade me to continue recommencing my prayers. He also gave me some rules to follow regarding the scruples which so fearfully tortured my soul. Our Lord gave me the grace to obey my confessor and to disregard those imaginary sins which heretofore oppressed me. In this way Satan was overthrown by my obedience. All my disquietude vanished like smoke, and calm and joy returned into my heart.

Filled with confidence and peace of mind, I received our Divine Saviour in Holy Communion, and found myself inundated with consolations. Signal graces were also granted me when later I assisted at Holy Mass. At the moment of consecration, it required much effort on my part to contain myself so that those around me would not notice my transports of joy. I now became continually aware of the presence of God.

2

My FATHER at this time entrusted me into the care of his two sisters who had a dressmaking shop, so that I should learn to work, but even this did not distract me from my interior conversations with God. I constantly conversed with our Lord in the secret of my soul. I also made frequent Spiritual Communions which exercise lighted in my heart a fire of divine love that transported me so strongly even in the midst of my employment, that I found it difficult not to show my emotions. Fortunately, my aunt had placed me in a corner close to her in the workshop. Remaining there as if in a small cell of my own, and separated from the other young people, they did not disturb my peace nor notice the workings of grace in my soul.

Shortly thereafter I was granted the favor of being received into the Congregation of the Most Blessed Virgin in which my aunt was one of the superiors. Having completed the term of probation, I was duly admitted by the Council and made my Act of Consecration. Oh, how sweet was that day to me. The ceremony reminded me of my first Communion. I was, as on that day, dressed all in white, and carried a large, lighted wax candle. This congregation had been established for working girls. No vows were taken, but the society had its rules that tended to preserve piety in the hearts of the young women who were members. Every two weeks the superior would give us a useful instruction.

Our Lord, having nourished me now for quite a long

time with the milk of consolations, wished to give me a more solid nourishment in order to strengthen my soul. He made me pass from Thabor to Calvary. The Divine Saviour withdrawing His consolations now abandoned me to spiritual dryness and interior aridity. This state seemed very strange to me. Alas, not to feel the love of God! Not having had very much experience in the spiritual life, I thought that if I applied myself very forcibly to meditation, I could in this way regain the taste of those delightful transports of Divine Love with which I had been favored in the past. My vehement efforts however were in vain and they only served to make me ill. When I disclosed the state of my soul to my confessor he was not surprised, but consoled me by saying that my former fervor would later return.

When, however, consolations did not come my way, I, ungrateful to my benefactor, grew lukewarm in the way of perfection and turned my heart to creatures. This brought me no peace, for although my faults were not grave in themselves, yet they were very displeasing to our Lord who demanded of me utmost generosity in His service.

At this stage I committed an imprudence which very greatly retarded my spiritual progress. Thinking that my confessor did not seem any longer concerned about my faults, I asked my father's permission to change confessor. Sympathizing with me, he consented, and himself approached my old confessor, whom I wanted to leave, who was also the pastor in our parish, and whom my father greatly esteemed, not without reason. The pastor suggested to him that perhaps I would be better off under the guidance of a certain confessor who then enjoyed a high reputation among the more devoted of the parish. The pastor, therefore, consented to my change to this new confessor, who was the Vicar General. But alas, I had occasion to repent for leaving my old confessor, because I learned that although the Vicar General had many years of experience in the ministry, he did not have any grace from God for my soul. He took me off frequent Communion. Undoubtedly, I deserved this for I was relenting in my spiritual exercises, but this Bread of the strong was necessary for me to combat my enemies.

Reaching the age of about seventeen, the attractions of the world now began to smile upon me. The priest would scold me for he could not stand anyone primping. He was seventy years old, but his eyes were excellent when it was a matter of discerning whether or not I dressed according to his taste. He did not want me to wear any ribbons, and his sharp eyes were quick to notice that I was wearing transparent stockings one Sunday. If I remained away from confession longer than one week, he was sure to come to our home to get me. What displeased me more than anything else however, was that he would, behind my back, inquire about my conduct from my older sister, and since I was not always too docile at home, and often caused her little troubles, she would promptly tell him everything, so that I found I was confessed in advance. After this priest would take me to task for something, he would finish by telling me that he was my best friend, for he would never scold me twice about the same thing.

This kind of guidance did not at all appeal to me. Yet it went on for two and a half years, during which time my life became very imperfect. Although I received some excellent advice from my new confessor I did not improve. I gave myself up to distractions and became lukewarm in the service of God. But what was yet more harmful to my soul was that I had given up the practice of meditation, that most useful method to help a soul conquer her passions.

After my mother's death, my elder sister was at the head of our house, but I was so proud that I would not always submit to her authority. A great many small disagreements followed in the household, and as I have said, she complained about it to my confessor, who was also hers. This placed me at a still greater disadvantage, and then my conscience too reproached me strongly for my infidelities to God whom I recognized to be so full of goodness. I then began to recall the happy days of my childhood when, faithful to God, I had been filled with His ineffable consolations, and I longed to return to Him, but I felt my soul chained down by its passions. But finally I decided to have recourse to Mary, my tender Mother, to whom I had been consecrated, and whom no one ever invokes in vain.

. As Mary's beautiful feast of the Purification was drawing close, I prepared myself to celebrate it by making a novena. Then I went before her altar and burned a candle and soon I felt my heart entirely changed. I now realized that it was necessary for me to quit this confessor who had no grace to guide my soul and so I returned to my pastor who had been my first confessor.

"Oh, my Father," I said to him, "since I left you all virtue has fled far away from me." I then begged him to have the goodness to take over once more the care of my soul.

He received me as did the father of the Prodigal Son, that is, with great charity. Shortly afterwards I made an eight-day retreat, conducted by certain missionaries, at a convent. Oh, and it was, indeed, here that the divine mercy of God awaited me. I had prayed to the Blessed Virgin to obtain for me the grace to make a holy retreat, and this good Mother deigned once again to answer my prayers. Divine Grace worked so strongly on my soul that as I listened to the sermons I felt them making a most lively impression on me. I then made a general confession after which I saw all my sins very clearly, realizing how long I had refused to cooperate with the grace of God. Meditating on the wounds as I looked on my crucifix they seemed to reproach me for my infidelity. Then my heart was pierced with a most lively sorrow; my eyes were flooded with abundant tears, and there and then I vowed to God my inviolable loyalty.

Having come out of my retreat entirely converted, I was re-admitted to frequent Communion. I now became especially devoted to Mary realizing with what mercy this divine Mother had retrieved me from the abyss. And as my confidence in her was now very strong, I began to ask her to obtain for me the grace of a religious vocation. Mary undoubtedly heard my prayer again, for I soon began to experience a great longing to leave the world. But what was I to do? I dared not speak of it to my confessor.

One day as grace strongly urged me to follow my vocation, and not knowing how to go about it, I felt extremely pained, and in my dilemma I went to church. Kneeling before Mary's altar, I opened my heart to her, telling her of my great desire to become a nun, and of my troubles in regard to attaining this end. Mary immediately dispelled my worries. It so happened that there was a confessional box located close to the beautiful statue of Mary. This confessional was ordinarily occupied by one of her zealous servants, the very same priest about whom I have already spoken as being the one who had given me the role of a religious in the Catechism class, where also I was asked if I wanted to become a Carmelite. It was there, while I prayed before the statue of the Blessed Virgin, as I have mentioned, that suddenly I saw this good priest go into his confessional, and he seemed to beckon me to enter.

I cannot understand how he became aware of my worries, for I had never spoken to him about my soul, yet when I entered the Confessional he began to tell me everything that passed through my heart.

"You desire to become a religious, my child, and it seems

to you that to reach such a goal, you must scale a mountain. Isn't it true that I guess correctly?"

Overwhelmed at finding such a consoler, I opened my heart to him in all frankness. He, weighing seriously everything I told him, then and there declared that I had a real vocation to the religious life. Encouraged by his advice, I went immediately to find my confessor to whom I had not dared as yet to open my soul on this subject. When I told him of my desire to become a religious, he in turn answered as follows:

"I am in perfect accord with you on this matter. As for myself, I have always believed that you would become a nun."

His answer filled me with joy. A few days later he told me to plan entering the religious life sometime in the spring, as it seemed to him a favorable season for leaving. But, alas, I was to pass into the hands of another spiritual father who was not quite so quick to decide sending me to the convent. Instead he was to work for five years breaking down the wall of my pride and self-love with the hammer of mortification before he would find me worthy to dwell in the solitude of Carmel. This is how it happened.

My regular confessor was obliged to go to Paris for medical treatment for he was about to lose his sight. Since he knew that I needed an experienced guide to direct me in my vocation, he sent me to a learned priest — one who had proved himself of great service to the religious communities of the diocese which he visited often. He was, moreover, particularly enlightened on the subject of the interior life, and he was known for this throughout the city. Mothers felt very much flattered when their daughters went to consult him. He was continually engaged in sending young ladies to the convents, and it was generally known that none of those whom he sent had ever returned to the world.

I approached him and told him that I wanted to be a Carmelite nun. He received me with much charity and encouraged me to pursue my vocation. However, he told me that he was not willing to undertake the direction of my soul until he had first consulted our Lord about this in prayer.

In the meantime, this new confessor's counsels proved of so much benefit to me that I begged him to be willing to assume charge of my soul even after my old confessor had returned from Paris. Then after considering this for some time, he gave me the following answer:

"My daughter, I take charge of your soul for the glory of God and for the salvation of your soul."

These words inspired me with great confidence in his direction. Then wishing to sound me out, he asked me to submit to him in writing an account of the way our Lord had in the past directed my soul, as likewise a brief résumé of my present dispositions. After I had sent him this written account, he made me draw up for myself a rule of life.

Then when some time had elapsed, I begged him to see about my being received into some convent to which he replied:

"Oh, my daughter, you have only begun to make war on your passions. They must be overcome."

As I was very eager to become a Carmelite nun and would have passed through fire had this been necessary in order to become one, I therefore began with renewed fervor to strive after perfection. And as the advice which this priest gave me continued to make the deepest impression on my heart, I took care not to forget any of it.

He began by warning me against those small weaknesses so common among many devout souls.

"My daughter," he would say to me, "do not consult, as many pious persons do, some thirty-six different spiritual directors. If you desire me to be truly your father, I desire that you be truly my daughter. Be simple as a child. It is here that you must tell all and not elsewhere, for otherwise it is nothing but a sad waste of time, and is worth nothing. Never speak about your confessor nor about your mortifications. Go straight to God in a spirit of faith. Do not allow your soul to swerve from its course, for all back-sliding is only so much straw for the fires of purgatory. Endeavor to know yourself and to know God, for the more you will know Him, the more also will you love Him. Be always cheerful and not like those sad people who in carrying the yoke of the Lord seem to be carrying a burden. Oh, my daughter, how beautiful is the road which our Lord has chosen for you to follow. Look to the end! Prepare yourself well for the great designs God has on your soul."

Such was the wise counsel which I received from this priest, which through God's grace bore fruit in my soul. He loaned me books which treated of prayer and of the interior life, and also biographies of the saints. All these spiritual helps nourished my soul, and enkindled in my heart an ever more lively longing to embrace the religious life. But whenever I expressed this desire to my confessor, and told him of my longing to leave the world and become a Carmelite nun, he would simply answer in a very unconcerned manner: "My daughter, the habit does not make the monk."

By this answer I understood that there was still work ahead of me. I prayed constantly to the Blessed Virgin, my dear protectress, to allow me to become a Carmelite nun in one of the houses where she was much beloved. I also prayed very much to the glorious St. Joseph, and asked him for the gift of prayer. In order to obtain this precious grace, and all the other graces of which I had such great need, especially that of becoming a Carmelite, I would make small pilgrimages to his shrines. In his honor I would eat dry bread for breakfast on

Wednesdays and also on Saturdays in honor of the Blessed Virgin. Thus I constantly practiced a great devotion to the Holy Family, as I became entirely taken up with thoughts of Jesus, Mary and Joseph. "Oh, blessed family," I would say, "if I had had the good fortune to live at the time when you dwelt upon earth, believe me, no matter in what country you would have lived, I would have gone out to find you in order to have the honor of being your servant in the form of a little domestic."

So when my director loaned me a book on the Life of St. Teresa my joy was, indeed, extreme, for in it I read about the promise our Lord made her on the occasion of founding her first monastery at Avila, saying that He Himself would dwell in that house, and that the Blessed Virgin would be watching the door on one side of the convent and St. Joseph on the other side. I now prayerfully pleaded to be allowed to have a place in Carmel for this reason above all others, that there I might live together with the Holy Family.

I repeatedly urged my confessor to help me in getting settled in a Carmelite monastery, but he still persisted in trying me by giving me the same evasive answers: "We will see about it. God's time has not yet arrived." Then one time he added, "Do you think, my daughter, that I want you to imitate those young women who rush off to a convent and soon afterwards come back home? No, my child, when I send you there, you will be prepared to stay."

Such were the answers he would invariably give me. Although they were very wise, they made me suffer a great deal because of my vehement desire to be a nun. In the meantime, while awaiting the honor of going to Carmel in order to serve the Holy Family there, Divine Providence furnished me with an excellent means of satisfying my longing to serve the Holy Family. Next door to our house there came to reside a poor family consisting of three persons, a poor laborer, his wife who was blind, and their little son, a boy about four or five years old. They were so impoverished, especially in the winter when the man was without a job, that I found their poor little house resembling the stable of Bethlehem. There they were, often without fuel and without bread. I saw here an excellent opportunity to honor in the persons of these poor neighbors the Holy Family itself and I resolved therefore not to remain idle in their regard. By the grace of God I began with great affection to render them every service which their sad condition demanded from the time they moved next door to our house until the time I entered Carmel. Since my meager financial resources did not permit me to satisfy all their needs, the Holy Family, whom I served in their persons, granted me the grace of so eloquently pleading their cause among people whom I knew in order to secure further help for them that no one was able to refuse me.

All my happiness now consisted in visiting them, and in instructing them in the practice of our religion, which their extreme poverty undoubtedly led them to neglect. I induced them to go to confession and also made the husband attend an eight-day retreat in a religious house where these retreats were conducted. But if I loved this poor family, I was also loved by them, so much so that when the husband would be mean to his wife, which happened from time to time, I was called in to be the judge of the matter and restore peace.

Despite my unworthiness, the Holy Family knew well how to recompense me with abundant graces for the service which I rendered to this poor family. I will declare, for the glory of God alone, that my soul made rapid progress in virtue. Here is what our Lord gave me the grace to practice in a more special manner during the five years I spent as an aspirant under the direction of my new guide, who had me take a vow of chastity which I renewed on all the Feasts of the Blessed Virgin, and a promise of obedience to his orders.

The virtues which I strove to acquire were mortification, prayer, humility, obedience and charity towards my young companions, and our Lord gave me the grace to succeed.

3

I ALWAYS had a great attraction for the exercise of prayer, but knowing that I could not become a daughter of prayer without being a friend of mortification, I worked with great courage to acquire this virtue and to destroy my passions. To help me succeed, I decided to keep a daily record of my faults and also of my acts of mortification, for which purpose I always kept at my side two little strings of beads. The string of my mortifications was composed of fifteen beads in honor of the fifteen mysteries of the holy rosary and I believe that often when night came I was able to offer Mary a crown complete, with every bead marked for her. From whatever was pleasant for me to see, I would deliberately turn my eyes away. Similarly, if I felt a strong desire to say something, I would not say it, and so forth.

I made my general examination of conscience and a particular one with the aim of conquering my predominant passion which was pride, and I received the grace to subdue it. Having thus given myself unreservedly to our Lord, who never allows Himself to be outdone in generosity, I will now relate in what manner our Lord now gave Himself entirely to me. I had already during the course of my life on several occasions been granted extraordinary favors, yet if I may thus express it, these were but samples of the heavenly favors with which He was to enrich my soul in such profusion. It was during Holy Communion which I now had the happiness to receive three times each week and on Sundays that our Lord would communicate Himself intimately to my soul.

Since my director had commanded me to tell him with the simplicity of a child everything that transpired within me, I gave him a written account of these supernatural happenings. However, on learning of them, my confessor did not appear at all surprised.

"My daughter," he said, "does not your soul belong to God? Let then this good Master do as He wills in His own house."

As time went on and as these interior words of our Lord and His heavenly communications continued to be showered on me, I in turn was faithful in continuing to submit written accounts of them to my confessor for thus I knew I would be preserved from illusion. My director, however, never spoke to me of these things which pleased me very much for feeling myself unworthy of such divine favors, to speak about them to anyone, even my father confessor, caused me extreme confusion.

Then one day, as I was handing my director one of these notes, it occurred to me that my humiliation would be much deeper were I to read aloud the contents of the letter I wrote, which in spite of my unworthiness, set forth such wonderful proofs of our Lord's affection for me. I told my confessor what was going through my mind and he ordered me to begin reading the account, which I did, at the cost of excessive violence to myself.

But our Lord desired at this time to counteract these extraordinary graces by a stroke of His mercy, for an unbroken succession of celestial favors might have caused in my soul sentiments of vanity. One day after Holy Communion, I beheld what seemed to me to be a wall, about to fall and crush me. Although it is quite a long time ago since this took place, I will explain as best as I can what happened in my soul. Our Lord told me not to fear anything. I understood that the falling wall would crush only my self-love. I have since then realized that what I saw represented a long series of humiliations and mortifications, very distasteful to self-love, which was to be the road on which our Lord would soon have me enter.

Since without grace we can do nothing, our divine Saviour embued me at this time with a strong desire for sufferings and humiliations. Answering the call of grace, I now actually began to pray for humiliations in order that the wall of my pride which prevented perfect union with God might be entirely destroyed, and that the violet of humility which attracts Jesus to people's hearts might now bloom within me. I made my desires known to my confessor and I prayed him not to spare me.

"Father," I said to him, "do not listen to the cries of nature. Help me conquer my pride."

Since he was never in any haste to form conclusions, he waited, undoubtedly, to see if this was a mere passing fervor, too common among young people, or if it was really the work of God. But, finally, seeing that our Lord continued to give me this desire to purify my soul of all the faults of pride into which it had fallen in the past, my director ended by telling me:

"My daughter, I believe our Lord wants you to walk outside the usual way, and is leading you in an extraordinary manner. Therefore, go before the Blessed Sacrament and reflect in His presence what you could do to humiliate yourself. Choose whatever would cause you the deepest humiliation."

Then began for me the painful voyage on the road of humiliation. Each time that I went to see my director to ask him for books, or to return those he ordinarily loaned me, he always had the charity to serve me a large plate of humiliations. But grace never left me. At times I had to beg him to continue the good work which he was doing.

"Ah, well," he would then say to me, "what does our Lord ask of you today? Have you any favor to ask of me?"

Since extreme simplicity was one of my characteristics, and since our Lord gave me the grace to walk in this way, I would think of a great many things which, in my judgment, would cause me deep humiliation. I knew, of course, that most of them were not practical, yet I saw that the mere mention of them, as also asking my confessor's permission to perform them became in itself the keenest humiliation of all, and therefore I would begin to stammer my suggestions. At times when my confessor would discern how deeply it hurt me to tell him everything, he would scold a little but always with sweetness:

"Be as simple as a little child," he would say to me. "Look at a child, and take note that he says everything that comes to his mind without examining it."

Then, after weighing my suggestions, he would allow me to perform those acts of humiliation which seemed practical to him. As for the others, he would pretend at first to give his consent, and after he was assured of my willingness to perform them, he would later forbid me to carry them out.

"Oh, my father," I would sometimes exclaim, "how much it costs me to walk in this path!"

"My daughter," he would answer, "if it costs you to be humiliated, I assure you that it costs me also to be obliged to humiliate you. But have courage."

After I had trodden my pride under foot, our Lord filled my soul with spiritual consolations. However, I must add that this was quite necessary for me, for without this all-powerful grace, I would never have been able to walk on a road so replete with pain. Whenever I would feel inspired to perform some unusual act of humility, I experienced within me so strong a movement of grace, that it was impossible for me not to perform that mortification without fear of being unfaithful.

"Let us go," I would say to encourage myself, "only one heroic act is necessary to bring about a victory. I can do all things in Him that strengthens me." I would then feel sure that grace demanded this act of mortification from me. Therefore, in spite of all the repugnance which I experienced, I would ask my director often again to nourish me with this bread so disagreeable to the taste of nature. He sent me a few times to the house of two pious young ladies where I found occasions of practicing humility. One of my friends complained to me that a certain person had said something humiliating to her. "Oh," I then answered her, "you are very fortunate to find humiliations already prepared for you. There are some souls who have to look for them."

But during this time of trial, I found strength and consolation in visiting our good Saviour present in the Most Blessed Sacrament, where I went especially at mid-day when He was more alone than at other times, and there opened my soul to Him.

Then, too, I had a very great devotion to the Sacred Heart of Jesus, to whom I often made acts of reparation. I implored Him to break the bonds which held me in the world so that I could take my flight to a Carmelite monastery.

Next I would go to that chapel where I had previously received marvelous graces concerning my religious vocation and, kneeling at the feet of the Blessed Virgin's statue, I would pour out my heart to her as does a child to the one it loves. I used to pray to her continually: "Behold," I would say to her, "look around and see, my companions are one after another getting married. When will the time then come, my mother, when you will give me your Son for my spouse, since you know I want no other but Him?"

To this kind mother I also made a novena asking her to obtain for me the cure of a physical ailment. She promptly granted me my favor in thanksgiving for which I had fifteen masses offered in honor of the fifteen mysteries of the holy rosary, as I had promised.

While awaiting to be received into the Carmelite convent, I still continued to work at my pious aunt's dressmaking shop where she employed quite a few young women. It now fell to my lot to assume the role of mistress or spiritual directress among several of these companions, who began now to consult me. Noticing that although through the grace of God I practiced virtue, and yet I appeared ever cheerful and contented, as my director had counseled, these young women would approach me with much confidence. Since they would consult me on all their little qualms of conscience and on the practice of devotion, I taught them how to make mental prayer and how to exercise various acts of virtue.

Miserable sinner that I was, since I had received so much from God, it was only just that I should give myself in charity towards the others. In a short time, one of these young persons made so much progress that she greatly surpassed her little directress, and in fact she entered religion, becoming a nun even before I did.

Our conversations always centered around our Lord, the Blessed Virgin, St. Joseph and the practice of various virtues. Then reflecting on the way they would consult me, who myself had such a great need of counsel, I feared that, perhaps, this was contrary to the virtue of humility. I, therefore, spoke of this to my director, but he advised me to continue the work I had begun since the virtue of these young companions would serve to stimulate my own spiritual progress. I was, therefore, at peace, and never mentioned to my companions what passed through my heart, keeping the secret as my own.

It was easy for me to teach them how to practice prayer because I enjoyed a great facility in performing mental prayer by simply considering our Lord present in the midst of my soul. In fact, this presence of the divine Saviour, for a certain period of time, was so real and sensible, that it seemed to me that I actually saw Him in the center of my heart.

It now happened that one of these companions was stricken with a very extraordinary illness. Seeing that the remedies which the physicians prescribed brought her no relief, I believe that I had an interior light that if we had recourse to the Blessed Virgin, the patient would be cured of her strange malady. I, therefore, had her wear a miraculous medal around her neck, and we then made a novena to the Most Blessed Virgin, after which the young lady was entirely cured of her illness. Consequently, these graces which we received from Mary inflamed us with love for her.

I prayed to her continually to shatter the bonds which held me captive in the world. Often too I burned candles in front of her altar, and made novenas in preparation for her feasts, offering her garlands of artificial flowers and other ornaments. In fact, I did everything possible to honor and touch her maternal heart so that she would give me her Son for my spouse.

Although my poor prayers must have fallen short of pleasing so great a Queen of Heaven, yet she did not remain indifferent to them. She began auspiciously to lift one of the obstacles which somewhat prevented me from leaving the house of my father.

As I have already mentioned, my mother died when I was twelve years old, and my elder sister, since that time, was in charge of the household. My good father who thought of nothing else except of God and of his employment, worked in peace at his trade of locksmith. Never thinking about re-marrying, his life truly resembled that of St. Joseph. He went to Mass every morning and to Benediction in the evenings whenever he could. In spite of his hard manual labor, he observed all the fasts and abstinences prescribed by the Church, and approached the sacraments with a very lively faith and much fervor. He also carried with great patience some very trying crosses which God had sent him.

At this time my father became very worried, for my elder sister who had been managing our house was struck with a lingering illness, and my dear father had the idea that I wanted to leave him in order to embrace the religious life. He could not reconcile himself to the thought of entrusting his household to a hired domestic servant, and he would tell me about his worries, saying that he feared that some day I would fly away from him. I myself never spoke openly to him about my vocation because my confessor, still trying me, gave me little hope in spite of my longings, so that I did not know when he would grant me permission to leave for Carmel. In the meantime, my respectable father made the following overture. He spoke about his worries to the pastor, to whom I had already confided also my own longings to become a nun. This pastor who loved my father very much, and who used to say that he was his best parishioner, undoubtedly advised him to remarry. My father's disposition was somewhat timid and aloof and I think he was embarrassed at the pastor's idea. However, taking himself full initiative in the matter, the pastor interested himself in my father's remarriage, and finally, by the grace of God and Mary's intercession, he found my father an excellent wife. We received her very well, all of which made my father extremely happy.

After that I received my director's permission to speak openly of my intentions to enter Carmel, for until then I was not free to even speak of it either to my father or to my aunts. At last I felt that I was approaching the end of all my troubles and that the door of Carmel would soon open to me.

[27]

4

MY AUNT, for whom I worked, decided to take a trip to the Carmelites of Le Mans, in order to assist at the blessing of a new building and to visit in that convent a Carmelite nun who was very dear to her. My aunt invited me to accompany her on the trip, and I, overcome with joy, pressed my confessor to allow me to profit by this opportunity to realize my hope of becoming a Carmelite nun.

My confessor consented, and gave me a letter of introduction to the Reverend Mother Prioress. He also told me that if the nuns at the Carmel of Le Mans could receive me, I had his blessing to stay there. Leaving with my aunt, we arrived on the eve of the dedication ceremony, and were very well received by the Carmelites there. The following day I assisted at the blessing of the new refectory and cemetery, and also witnessed a ceremony of Investiture scheduled for that day. Because of the dedication ceremony, the ordinary rule governing strict enclosure of the monastery was suspended, and we were therefore allowed to visit inside the cloister. I entered one of the cells and there saw those dear Carmelites, some of whom came from my part of the country. Indeed, nothing could have been more pleasant for me than this visit to Carmel.

Finally, I was privileged to see the Reverend Mother Prioress to whom, on the evening before, I had handed my confessor's letter of introduction, and I told her of my great desire to enter Carmel. But she answered saying that she had been forbidden by the bishop to accept any more postulants because the convent was already too small, and all the cells were filled. I consulted her, nevertheless, about my vocation, telling her about my interior dispositions. After weighing my words, she told me that she felt certain our Lord had chosen me to become a daughter of Carmel, despite my unworthiness. She further explained to me the Rules of the Order and expressed her regrets at not being able to admit me, but as the bishop was absent from the diocese at the time, and she had no way of reaching him to seek a dispensation, she could not receive me. The Prioress then spoke to me in highest terms of praise about the Carmel at Orleans, from which house she herself had come to make the foundation at Le Mans, and urged me to make my application for admittance there.

In the meantime I felt something at the bottom of my heart which made me understand that I had no vocation for the house at Le Mans and now, obliged to return to the world which seemed to me insupportable, I asked my confessor to write to the Carmelites at Orleans about whom the good Mother had spoken to me, or else to the Carmelites at Blois. But he was in no haste to do so. However, since I continued to urge him he must have wearied of me. His evasive answers such as, "We will see," or "God's time has not yet arrived," made me suffer very deeply.

Finally, one day, I made a visit to the chapel of St. Martin. It happened, I believe, to be his feast-day for his relics were exposed for veneration, and I kissed them very fervently. I had already received Holy Communion that morning in his honor, although I had only slight knowledge of the life of this remarkable saint at the time. In fact, I did not even know what parts of France he had evangelized; however, that mattered very little.

Steeped in anguish, I formulated a simple but fervent prayer, which was somewhat as follows: "Oh, my good St. Martin, see how I suffer. I long to give myself to God by embracing the religious life, but nobody wants to help me, or receive me. Oh, I am certain that if only you were now on earth, your charitable heart would be moved with pity at what I endure. You surely would do something for me!"

At last I begged him to receive me in his diocese if he had any Carmelite religious there. Confiding to him all my troubles, I prayed to him, with a heart penetrated with sorrow and confidence.

In spite of my unworthiness, he heard my prayer, for I do not doubt that it is he who obtained for me the grace of entering the Carmelite Convent at Tours, for I never expressed any wish to my confessor to enter the cloister at Tours, since I never even knew that there were any Carmelites there until I was actually received by them, as I will relate later.

Our Lord in the meantime inclining my soul ever more to accept this life of sacrifice in the religious state, conferred on me one day after Holy Communion a vision. As the Divine Saviour gathered the powers of my soul into his divine Heart, it seemed to me that I saw many persons who were linked together with a golden chain, each one carrying a cross. These were, undoubtedly, religious souls because I recognized among them one of my friends who was a nun. It seemed to me that I also was chained together with these souls and I begged our Lord to give me a cross likewise. He then made me understand that it was necessary for me to conform my will to His and to await the accomplishment of His designs with resignation, for this constituted my cross for the present.

"But," He then added, "when you enter religion, I will give you another cross to carry."

This promise remained engraved in my memory so deeply that when I became a postulant at Carmel, finding myself a little sick for a few days, shortly after entering, I said to myself: "Look, maybe this is the cross our Saviour had promised me."

But poor simpleton that I was, this sickness was a mere straw to carry in comparison with the cross which the Saviour was reserving for me after my religious profession. I am convinced now that the Work of Reparation which the Lord later revealed to me was, indeed, the cross He had predicted. I found it in the Sacred Heart of Jesus, for it was in this furnace of love that He did first speak to me of that Work of Reparation which was to cost me so many sighs, so many prayers and so many tears.

Having a great devotion to the Sacred Heart of Jesus, I was always meditating on it, and taught my companions to also honor it. As my sister was still sick, I asked her to have a novena of Masses offered in reparation for the outrages committed against the Heart of Jesus in the Sacrament of His love to obtain her cure, if it were the will of God. She consented, and I had these Masses said in the chapel of the nuns of the Visitation, itself, choosing this particular place because it was to a nun of the Visitation Order that our Lord revealed the Devotion to His Sacred Heart, and also because the main altar in this chapel was especially dedicated to the Sacred Heart of our divine Saviour.

I myself assisted at all these Masses at which I received from our Lord extraordinary favors, an account of which I noted down in writing and submitted it, as always, to my confessor. However, I did not keep a copy of any of these notes for myself, for by now I was concerned in only one thing and that was to correspond with the immense love of our Saviour shown me in His Sacred Heart. The case being such I do not remember all that took place, but I do recall even now that my soul was at that time entirely wrapt in God. I moreover distinctly remember that Our Lord also showed me a cross and explained to me that upon it He crucified all those whom He had espoused to Himself. I do not know whether I was frightened at this but I recall that He then added a few words saying something like this: "Be consoled, my daughter. You will be crucified only after the nails penetrate my flesh before entering yours."

Our Lord wanted, undoubtedly, to tell me by these words that having Himself first undergone the torments of the cross, He had thus lessened their bitterness for His disciples who were destined to carry it after Him.

After this, our Lord for a second time favored me with a special kind of prayer that was truly blissful. However, He made me understand that this grace would be taken away from me, but that later on He would again confer this gift upon me. As far as I can remember I fell into a state of dryness for our Lord made me pass from Thabor to Calvary, according to His pleasure and the needs of my soul. However, since at this period I was better acquainted with the ways of God than I had been during my childhood, I went through this painful trial without sustaining any injury to my soul.

I want now to speak of a certain grace which our Lord conferred on me at this time, which I esteemed more highly than any of the supernatural favors and consolations which it had pleased Him to send me from time to time. In his mercy, the Saviour gave me the grace to practice charity by giving alms, and to allow me to serve several of the poor who were sick, implanting within me a great desire to alleviate their needs. Since I had a small purse of my own with which I was free to do as I pleased without bothering my father, I made money contributions to the poor, telling myself that at one time the poor person was our Lord, and at another time, our Blessed Lady. In the meantime I felt that this Blessed Mother would certainly reward me by finding me a place in her Order of Mount Carmel.

It was providential that at this time there came to live close to our house a young woman who had taken sick shortly after her marriage. In her long-drawn-out sickness I had the grace to help prepare her for her death. I placed a picture of the Blessed Virgin near her bed which, undoubtedly, obtained for her grace in her sad and painful final combat. Being still young, I had not had much experience in the presence of death and this poor sick person whom I encouraged with words of consolation wanted to have me always at her side. However, God sustained and helped me.

One time they sent for me during the night to ask if I thought she was going to die soon. I told her that, indeed, she was in her last extremity and that God would soon call her to Himself. I do not know if it was that night but all of a sudden she was frightened at a certain object which was, undoubtedly, the angel of darkness who came to tempt her in her last agony.

"I see," she said, "a large black cat at the foot of my bed."

As for me, I did not see anything. I then sprinkled her bed with holy water.

"I still see it," she insisted. After that I made a second aspersion and the object was obliged to flee. Then as we all were praying for this good sick person, she expired in front of our eyes, having already received the last Sacraments with edifying dispositions.

And now God permitted that it should devolve on me and a friend of mine to shroud this dead person, which act of charity I found very repugnant. But since there was no other person to render this service our Lord helped me to perform it, although I was very much frightened in the presence of death which I had never before seen so closely.

In this manner our Lord in His mercy gave me a means of atoning for my many sins, which must have been the real cause holding back my entrance into a religious community. But finally, our Lord's good moment was at hand! I began to pray to all the saints to intercede for me and I also had recourse to our holy mother, St. Teresa, of whom my father had a picture in his room. Often when seated at table I would look without stopping at this great saint, and sometimes became more concerned in her than in my dinner.

My father who by now knew that I wanted to be a Carmelite nun would sometimes speak to me about it while we were at dinner. One day he really made me laugh by repeating one of those stories which people in the world like to tell, exaggerating the austerities of Carmelite nuns. Raising the topic of the kind of bed I would be required to sleep in at Carmel, he said: "Dear child, if the sheets of the Carmelites are nailed at the four corners, as some people say, how will you be able to rest or go to sleep in a bed like that?" But such things were the least of my worries.

I was not satisfied with praying to our holy mother, St. Teresa, alone. While reading her life, I jotted down the names of her confessors, spiritual directors, and all the holy persons who had helped her launch her great reform. Of these I composed a litany without even stopping to examine whether they were all canonized. I placed the name of St. John of the Cross the first on this list, followed by others to whom I had most devotion, imploring all these advocates to plead my case and to open for me at last the gates of the Carmelite cloister.

It turned out that they really answered my prayer of confidence in them for it was actually on the Eve of the Feast of All the Saints of Carmel, immediately after first vespers, that they introduced me into the enclosure of the Carmelite monastery which I had so long desired.

But there was yet one last trial awaiting me. My director fell ill and he was unable to hear confessions. I immediately chose another priest to whom I intended to go until my regular confessor would recover. But God was to conduct me through a very extraordinary way, as always. My confessor, now sick, sent for me. When I arrived he made me understand that as long as I did not have anything of a serious nature bothering my conscience I should continue receiving Holy Communion without going to confession. Furthermore he made me understand that as long as through the grace of God I committed only small faults of frailness, he preferred that I should efface these by an act of contrition rather than expose myself by going to another confessor who would not have the grace to direct me and who perhaps would do me more harm than good.

This was all good and well, but how was I, in the meantime, to get on in the one great business of my life, that of entering a convent, unless I had a priest willing and able to undertake arranging the various steps necessary to settle my vocation? Surely, it was out of the question for me to press this poor sick man to interest himself with the matter of my reception into a convent. What then was I to do in the meantime, while he remained sick in bed, became the burning problem that now consumed me who longed to fly over the mountain of Carmel!

It was then that the most Blessed Virgin, my dear Mother, whom I had so much invoked, showed great mercy towards her little servant in spite of my unworthiness. I was inspired to make a pilgrimage to Our Lady of the Pines, who had already obtained for me a very signal favor from heaven. This chapel of Mary was six leagues from Rennes where I lived and it belonged in the parish of St. Didier. Since I knew the priest there very well, and since I also had one of my friends living there, I easily obtained permission to make this pilgrimage to honor Mary. I set out full of confidence, intending to ask this good Mother for the cure of my director as a proof of my vocation, and also to implore her to break my bonds, saying to her:

"Oh, I am like a bird in a closed cage who cannot in spite of every effort find even a little hole through which to escape and to fly away!"

It happened that I met a priest in the coach on my way there. Entering into conversation, I spoke to him about the glories of Mary. Seeing that he listened to me with interest, I went on to tell him about several incidents which showed her power with God, and I also acquainted him with the work of the Arch-Confraternity of the Holy Heart of Mary about which he had never heard. As we parted he assured me that he would on the following Sunday preach to his parishioners about the great graces to be obtained through the holy heart of Mary, which pleased me greatly for the holy Virgin was my delight and I loved to honor her according to my little capacity.

Finally I arrived at St. Didier. Having made my devotions in this church, our Lord, during my thanksgiving, deigned to communicate Himself to my soul, despite my unworthiness, and to speak to me on the topic of my vocation. But in order to make myself clear as to what I am about to report, it seems necessary for me first to mention that there was one particular worry which always asserted itself. I felt that entrance to Carmel might be refused me because my parents, not being rich, could give me only a small dowry of 600 francs.

Therefore, I had already on a certain occasion asked an ecclesiastic whom I knew to be wealthy to assist me, but he expressed his regrets saying that he was not able to oblige me because of certain considerable expenses which he had already incurred.

The supernatural communication which our Lord now conferred on me, which I am about to report, filled me with confidence, for I realized that I had perhaps failed somewhat in this respect towards Divine Providence. I believe that on this occasion He gave me a cross, and then as if to remove my anxiety He said to me: "Is not the vocation which I give you more than the dowry?" He then made me understand that if His infinite mercy had granted me the first grace which was of inestimable price, He was also powerful enough to grant me the second favor which was of much less worth. Our Lord then added: "Go to my Mother. It is through her that I will hear your petition."

Oh, never will I forget this happy promise! Full of faith and hope I continued on my pilgrimage to Mary's shrine which was located a quarter of a league from church. I soon found the miraculous statue of Mary standing in the center of the new chapel presently under construction, which was to replace the older one that had proved too small. With warm devotion, I deposited my small donation into a little box reserved for the offerings of the pilgrims. For nine successive days I made visits to the shrine, reciting the first part of the Rosary as I went there, the second part as I knelt before her statue, and finally the third part of the rosary on my way back. Oh, how I prayed to this good Mother asking her to break my bonds and to cure my confessor so that he would have the strength and energy to undertake the steps necessary to settle me in my religious vocation. I tasted, indeed, great sweetness praying before this consoler of the afflicted, to whom I opened my heart, and found that she was attentive to my pleadings.

Then, too, I received from Mary's divine Son very extraordinary favors during the course of this novena. I regret, however, that I did not preserve for myself a copy of these memoirs because of the glory they would now give to this most holy Virgin. As always, I sent an account of these favors to my confessor. I do remember, however, that on this occasion our Lord gave an explicit order to those concerned that they should, without any further delay whatsoever, attend to the matter of my vocation to the religious life. Writing an exact account of all that passed in my soul, I took this long letter before the statue of the Holy Virgin, asking her to bless it, and to touch the heart of my confessor for whom it was meant.

"Oh, good Mother," I said in simplicity, "I do not wish to spend another winter sewing garments of vanity. I want instead to be praising your divine Son. Behold, I deliver to you the tools of my trade," I added, and then deposited at the foot of her statue my scissors and my needles. At the end, having said everything I could think of to touch her tender heart, I bid her good-bye.

Returning to Rennes I went in search of my confessor whose health, thanks to Mary, was improved. I could see that the letter which I gave him made a deep impression on him, though he tried not to show this. During the week that followed there was ample evidence to indicate that he indeed applied himself wholeheartedly to the matter of my religious vocation, although he did this in secret. At first, appearing to oppose my vocation to Carmel, he suggested that I enter an order of hospital sisters.

What was I to do? So ardent was my desire to leave the world that I would have preferred to enter that order or any other rather than remain outside. I was not acquainted with any houses of Carmelites at all except, of course, the convent at Le Mans which was too crowded to receive me. As to there being any Carmelite convents in the city of Tours or at Morlaix, I had never so much as heard them mentioned.

So retiring to my little oratory where I kept a picture of St. Teresa and of St. John of the Cross I said to them: "Alas, you do not want any part of me!" Then the thought of my insufficient dowry came back to my mind, for our Lord had not forbidden me to think of it. He had only condemned my needless worry. In fact, our Lord had said to me: "Make an effort to enlist some help for yourself, for then heaven will help you."

I, therefore, decided to speak of my vocation and the problem of my dowry to the Vicar General, who had been my confessor once before during a period of two and a half years, when my spiritual life was very lukewarm, and when, undoubtedly, I often gave him cause for annoyance. Although this priest was now seventy-seven years old, his mental faculties were unimpaired and he was able to perform the duties of his ministry like a young priest. Of course, whenever he heard me speak of my wish to be a nun, judging from his reaction I gathered that he did not believe that I had any religious vocation at all. Meeting me casually on the street one day, some time back, he had rather dubiously inquired of me whether I really intended entering a convent. At the time I had evaded his questioning for I was unwilling to discuss the subject of my interior life right in the middle of the street, preferring to wait for a more favorable time and place to give him my confidence.

But as he was quite rich, I decided to ask him to help me with my dowry, and so first recommending this matter to the care of my protectress, the Blessed Virgin, I went one morning in search of this priest, and approached him in the confessional. Here I confidentially disclosed to him all my ardent longings to follow my vocation.

He, in turn, invited me to come to visit him at the rectory that afternoon, and from his manner of speaking I had no doubt but that he intended to put my vocation to a test. I saw all too clearly that he completely ignored the facts in the case, and all that I had confided to him about the multitude of humiliations and tests that had already bowed my poor soul down to the very ground uninterruptedly for five long years. But steeling myself to the ordeal, I went to pay my visit to the Vicar General in his house where our dear Saviour awaited me that He himself might crown my endless series of probes and tests. Respectfully kneeling at the feet of this venerable priest, I opened the subject of my vocation to him but he at once began to humiliate me in a most unpredictable fashion and with gestures of trying to push me away. It happened that my kneeling posture made me fall on my side, but, our Lord sustaining me with His powerful grace, I remained in that tiresome position, respecting the Will of God in that of His minister. Then taking his breviary, the priest began to read his office.

A while later he gave me the order to rise which I obeyed instantly. But there was yet another test awaiting me here by far more terrible than the first. The details of the mortifying episode that now took place I prefer to pass over in silence at this time for I have already in the past on several different occasions repeated to our Mothers in the cloister a full account of what transpired. This story, indeed, made them all laugh very heartily, for in point of truth it was so ridiculous that it proved very amusing, except of course for me who was the principal actor in the drama.

Let it be emphasized at this point, however, that only eight days had passed since my return from the pilgrimage, and the last time I had seen my director, he seemed to be practically decided to send me to the hospital sisters. I was, therefore, in a painful situation, since it was my ardent desire to live in the desert of Carmel. The spirit of retreat, of silence and of prayer had very much attraction for me, and I realized that if I entered the Order of hospital sisters I would be obliged to carry on active duties of nursing the sick and what was still more repugnant to me, shrouding the dead of whom I had a great fear.

Our good and merciful Lord now soothed my worry, and as He had promised to answer my petition through Mary's intercession He kept His promise. It was now the ninth day since my return from the pilgrimage to Mary's shrine. After receiving Holy Communion, I was overcome with the reality of God's infinite mercy, after which our Lord spoke to me as follows: "My daughter, I love you too much to abandon you any longer to suffer from this perplexity. You will not be a hospital sister. This is only a trial. You will be a Carmelite nun, and in fact, steps are right now being taken towards your reception." After that a very powerful voice repeated several times over and over again: "You will be a Carmelite!"

I believe also that our Lord added: "A Carmelite of Tours," but since I knew of no such place, nor had I ever even heard that there was a community of Carmelites in Tours, I began to fear that all this was perhaps an illusion. This the more so because by now I was quite convinced that my confessor had altogether given up the idea of ever sending me to the Carmelites.

However, since I was obliged by obedience to submit a written account of all supernatural communications to my confessor, writing down our Lord's words to me, I went, as was my custom, to deliver this little letter to my director. But oh, the infinite mercy of God! What was my surprise, when handing my note to the director, I heard him address me in the following words:

"My daughter, I want to tell you that you have just been accepted by the Carmelite nuns of Tours!"

What charming news was this! At last my day of happiness for which I had longed had arrived! Oh, how thankful I felt to our Lord! What gratitude, too, filled my heart for the Blessed Virgin who so promptly answered the prayers I addressed to her during my pilgrimage! For, indeed, it was that letter I wrote at the shrine of Our Lady of the Pines, asking her to bless it, so that I might touch the heart of my confessor for whom it was meant, that turned the tide. I later learned that when my director read that letter, he at once wrote to the Prioress of the Carmelites of Tours, and this Reverend Mother, full of charity, had answered him immediately saying that she would receive me.

But what was also quite remarkable was the fact that this Prioress, having heard that there lived in Rennes a priest who prepared many subjects for the religious life, had planned to write him to ask that he send her a postulant, if any were available. She was consequently very astonished to have a letter from this priest, proposing a postulant, without having written him first.

I now asked myself why our Lord in such a marked manner indicated His choice of Tours, which is sixty leagues from my home town, when there were Carmelites at Nantes and at Morlaix, which were located much closer? When I inquired of my confessor if he had ever had any dealings with the Carmelites of Tours, he told me that he had not. I then asked him if he had ever visited the Tours cloister, for he was accustomed frequently to visit religious houses in his travels. Again he assured me that he had never been at the Tours convent, though he had thought of visiting their house when he was in that city some time ago.

How then did it come about that I should be proposed by my confessor to the Carmel of Tours rather than to the one at Orleans, about which I learned from the Prioress at Le Mans, and about which I pressed my confessor so repeatedly? The answer to the mystery is this—that evidently the great St. Martin had not forgotten the prayer I had addressed to him in his chapel on his feast day where I received Holy Communion in his honor, and where also I had venerated his holy relics. For I begged this saint very ardently to find me a nook in the diocese of which he had been the bishop, if there were any religious of the Carmelite Order there. But there was yet another remarkable sign pointing to St. Martin's intercession in my behalf for by a special stroke of Providence, the Prioress deferring my entrance for two months, I left the city of Rennes on the very feast of St. Martin, being November 11. Is not this proof that evidently the Blessed Virgin whom I had so much entreated during my pilgrimage condescended to arrange all this in connection with St. Martin?

There remained now only the question of my still insufficient dowry for although the Prioress of the Tours Carmel in her selflessness and charity, asked for a modest enough sum as the entrance dowry, still this exceeded very much my small means. As I have already said, although my father was a successful master locksmith and did a prosperous business, he had also to endure many reverses. My elder sister continued to be sick. Furthermore, when my brother who was drafted into the army was unable to afford paying for his replacement by another, my father and my aunts were obliged to raise two thousand francs to defray this expense. For that reason our family found it impossible to give me more than six hundred francs for my dowry.

Then came to pass what our Lord had told me when He said that He who had given me a religious vocation could also provide me with a dowry. Evidently too, the Blessed Virgin wished to reward me for the small gift I made her towards the erection of her shrine. Quite unexpectedly, a young lady whose name was Mary, with whom my director had me practice the virtue of mortification, and who was also being prepared by him for future entrance into a religious community, took it upon herself, as an angel of virtue, to supply generously the sum that was still wanting. And now also the good priest of whom I had already spoken, and who had made me endure such rude treatment at his hands, had the charity to offer me a little gift as well.

I now reflected to see what I could do to show my gratitude to the Blessed Virgin. Truly had our Lord told me: "Address yourself to my Mother for it is through her I will grant your petition," which words I shall always preserve in my memory. I therefore asked permission to return to the holy chapel of Our Lady of the Pines in order to thank Mary for her numberless favors, and thus fulfill the sacred duty of thanksgiving, by making a novena for this intention. Bidding her adieu at the end, I entrusted to her care the new religious state which I was about to embrace, which was to bind me so sweetly to herself and to her divine Son. In all simplicity I had asked her to give me for my spouse her own dear Son, and she consented. My heart had nothing more to desire, except to wait for the happy day of my spiritual nuptials.

Returning to Rennes, I looked forward to the day of my departure. As we were expecting a nun who was to pass through Rennes on her way to Tours, it was planned that I should make the trip under her care. However, she failed to arrive, and as I longed to depart without any delay, my dear father decided to leave work for a few days and himself accompany me on the trip to offer me to the Lord. Nor was it necessary for me to urge this upon him, for he was a man capable of any sacrifice once the Will of God was manifested to him.

It was with joy that I bade farewell to my family and to my country for although I loved them very much and was likewise loved by them, I nourished such a strong desire to serve the Holy Family at Carmel, that this prevented me from feeling any sadness at the thought of separation, otherwise so natural to all of us.

I also went to pay my respects to the confessor who had

directed me towards the fulfillment of my religious vocation. He assured me of my perseverance and with great confidence told me that the step I was about to make would settle me permanently. Then fearing that the extraordinary way through which our Lord was leading me might not always be in harmony with community life, he said to me:

"Daughter, try to walk the ordinary common road for indeed when a religious is conducted through extraordinary paths, she is thereby obliged to ask for extraordinary confessors which is not always convenient for a community to do." Finally giving me some useful parting advice, I also received his blessing and thus ended my secular life in the world.

5

ACCOMPANIED by my father, I left Rennes on November 11, 1839, it being the feast of St. Martin, my venerable protector. I reached the city of Tours on November 13, which happened to be the Vigil of the great Carmelite observance called the Feast of All the Saints of Carmel, arriving there about five o'clock in the evening. The special concurrence of dates impressed me as quite significant, for it appeared to me that St. Martin, on whose feast I was granted the grace to leave the world, was in a particular manner presenting me to all the saints of Carmel, since I arrived there on the Vigil of this solemnity. For indeed, I had prayed both to St. Martin and to these Carmelite saints asking them to admit me into their family, and they could not have given me a better proof of their charity towards me than to admit me into Carmel on such a beautiful feast-day.

Having no curiosity to go sight-seeing in the city, as soon as we left the coach, my father proceeded at once to escort me to the Carmelites. Embracing me for the last time, my father gave me his blessing, and with deep emotion told me that only the Will of God could have induced him to offer this sacrifice. Poor father, God shall certainly recompense your admirable resignation to His divine decrees!

Soon the enclosure door of Carmel opened, and my father entrusted me into the hands of a new family who stood at the threshold to receive me. If at that moment I made to God the sacrifice of a good father, our Saviour was in turn now to give me a good mother, who in her charity was to render my soul services of inestimable value. She was the reverend Mother Marie of the Incarnation, who was at that time prioress and also the mistress of novices. It seems to me that while still in the world, our Lord one day made me understand that the mother whom He had destined for me would have special grace to direct me in His ways. This is precisely what came to pass, as by degrees the prioress was given grace to understand my interior, a knowledge which did not penetrate her at once, but which was imparted to her only by degrees later on as God judged it convenient for His glory and for the salvation of my soul.

Having embraced my new sisters, the first thing the Reverend Mother did was to lead me before a statue of Mary, my good Mother, to thank her for admitting me into her holy house of Carmel, and to place myself under her powerful protection. Shortly afterwards it was the hour of recreation and I was invited to sing a few stanzas of a certain hymn. I needed no coaxing, and since I had sung this hymn repeatedly while awaiting the happy day of my entrance to Carmel, I began as follows:

> *Let us praise God, for I am in a shelter*
> *For which I have sighed a long time;*
> *Here I shall live for God in tranquillity*
> *Far from worldly things, far from worry.*

I had memorized about fifteen of these stanzas which I sang with such a gay and merry spirit that the prioress looking on seemed convinced that the little postulant from Brittany had certainly no leanings towards becoming melancholy. And in fact this candid and spontaneous gaiety which was one of my characteristics became for me already sure proof that I had a genuine vocation to Carmel, for I had learned that our holy mother, St. Teresa, said she never wanted persons inclined towards sadness or melancholy to be admitted into the Order.

The following day, on being taken to the choir to assist at the Divine Office, I had quite a ludicrous temptation, the only one which I can remember ever experiencing against my vocation. Seeing the hebdomadary, the chantresses, versiclers and certain other sisters go to the center of the choir at intervals to say a few words in Latin, and to make profound inclinations, and then return to their places only to be followed by others, I was frightened at so much ceremonial. I began to worry that I would never be able to learn how to do this, nor hope to remember when it would be my turn to go to the middle of the choir to perform these rubrics. Therefore, I told myself that it would be best for me to simply pack my small belongings and to return to Brittany. But then how could I do this, I asked myself, since I had but forty francs in my little purse which was insufficient for such a long trip and besides I suddenly recalled I had already turned over even that to the prioress. I therefore resigned myself to wait patiently and to see how things would turn out.

Next I was conducted to the confessional, another disappointment, for I saw there a piece of odd wire placed over the grill, according to custom. I was told that I would be obliged to speak through this to the confessor on the other side, but saying nothing, I decided to be patient again and wait to see how it would work out.

Lastly I was escorted to the novitiate, where I found images of the Divine Infant Jesus and of the Holy Family, the treasured objects of my heart. Soon this Holy Family for whom I had left the world in order to serve It at Carmel, and to whom I was especially devoted, helped me to find everything easy and agreeable. In fact, I felt right from the start as if I had lived at Carmel already many years. I now also experienced the feeling that one receives from God a vocation for a particular house as well as for a particular Order. Having become acquainted with the Carmel of Le Mans, for example, I did not feel called to live in that house, yet on the other hand, as soon as I had entered the Carmel of Tours, I felt that I was where God wanted me to be.

Shortly after entering the religious life, the God of Mercy communicated Himself to my soul and made me understand for what purpose He had called me to Carmel. I now learned from our Lord to hold in great esteem the sublime vocation which I proposed to embrace since its purpose was the glory of God and the salvation of immortal souls.

Until now all of the communications which I had received from our Lord had but one end and that was the sanctification of my own soul. Therefore, until now I had worked only for myself, being charged with the task of pursuing my own spiritual perfection.

However, upon entering Carmel which is devoted to the needs of the Church, the glory of God and the salvation of souls, our Lord now inspired me with the spirit of sacrifice and zeal for the salvation of souls. This was, indeed, sublime virtue and unselfishness, but until then I knew nothing of them.

Our Lord now communicated Himself to me on this subject asking me to make an act of complete self-sacrifice to God for the accomplishment of His designs. This first call of our Lord in which He asked me to offer myself in self-surrender, I still consider as the very basis and foundation of the Devotion of Reparation to His Holy Face, which He was later to reveal to me. However, before our Lord spoke openly to me of the Holy Face Devotion, which He was later to entrust to me, He first waited until my superiors, as it were, gave me their permission to make this act of self-sacrifice to God for the accomplishment of His designs.

This communication of our Lord remained deeply engraved in my soul, but since I did not preserve any written account of it, I can now make it known only in substance. One day after receiving Holy Communion our Lord manifested Himself to my soul. It seemed to me that He was accompanied by an angel. I was then shown a multitude of souls who were falling into hell. Our Lord then said to me that He desired that I offer myself entirely to Him to endure everything He might send me for the accomplishment of His designs. Furthermore, He wanted me to resign whatever merits I might acquire in my new career to Him for this same purpose, that His designs might be fulfilled. At the same time He made me comprehend that He Himself would look after my interests, that He would allow me to share His merits, and that He would Himself become the director of my soul. The angel at His side urged me to consent to so magnificent a proposal, and he seemed envious at my good fortune. He seemed in a fashion to regret not having a body, making me understand that whereas it was possible for me to acquire merit, he was unable to do this. Furthermore, this heavenly spirit told me that if I gave my consent to our Lord's proposal, the holy angels would surround my bed at my death and would defend me from the snares of the demon.

I do not know exactly if our Lord Himself told me that I must first secure my superior's permission before making this special act of self-abandonment, but I do know for certain that although I had a great desire to make this act at once, I did not do so right away, but instead I decided to wait until I could receive the advice of the Mistress who was also the prioress.

Writing down this communication, I handed it to the prioress similarly as I was accustomed to do while in the world with my confessor. Our good mother, who as yet did not know in what way our Lord was leading me, did not place much faith in what her little postulant had written her. In her wisdom, she answered me as follows:

"My child, the act of sacrifice to our Lord which you ask my permission to make is not an ordinary one. Since you are only a postulant, and as yet I have no right over you, I cannot counsel you to make this act. In fact, I do not permit it."

Since I had a very high esteem for obedience, I submitted respectfully to our prudent Mother's judgment. This did not prevent me, however, from feeling heartbroken. Returning to our Lord, I said to Him:

"My good Saviour, You can well see that it is obedience alone that prevents me from doing that which You ask of me. Since You see the very depths of my heart, You know that I give You all that I can give You."

For the time being, our Lord was satisfied with my willingness to obey. Yet during the period that followed He very many times urged me to repeat this same petition to my superiors. Finally, it was only after I had obtained permission to make the Act of complete self-abandonment, that our Lord communicated to me in its entirety the Work of Reparation through the devotion to His Holy Face, of which I will speak later on.

In the meantime our prudent Mother, seeing that her little postulant continued to tell her from time to time that our Lord communicated Himself to her soul, intending no doubt to test her spirit through obedience, to prove whether these communications were genuine, now forbade me to think about any of these favors. In the immediate days that followed I hardly ever heard any interior words at all, and our Lord, as it were, Himself aided me to defer to obedience.

But since I was at this time only an infant in the religious life of Carmel, our Lord now directed me to be entirely devoted to meditating on His Sacred Infancy. He traced out for me in my mind, for each day of the month, a course of devotional exercises intended to honor the Holy Childhood, which I now practiced with much consolation, and I think profit to my soul.

The following is a small extract which will give an idea of the exercises honoring all the mysteries of the Holy Childhood which were outlined for me by the Divine Infant Jesus in my mind:

MONTH OF THE HOLY INFANT JESUS

On the 15th of the month I began by celebrating the feast of the espousals of the Blessed Virgin with St. Joseph. On that day I asked them to accept me as their little house-servant in order that I may have the honor to wait on the Holy Infant Jesus.

The 16th, I dedicated to honoring the mystery of the Incarnation. During the nine following days, that is until the 24th, I adored the Holy Infant Jesus enclosed for nine months within Mary's chaste womb, finally accompanying the Blessed Virgin and St. Joseph on their journey to Bethlehem.

The 25th, I dedicated to celebrating the glorious Birth of the Infant Jesus.

The 26th, I dedicated to adoring the Infant Jesus in union with the shepherds.

The 27th, I dedicated to adoring the Holy Infant circumcised and given the name Jesus.

The 28th, I dedicated to worshiping the Divine Infant in company with the Three Holy Kings.

The 29th, I dedicated to honoring the mystery of the Presentation of Jesus in the Temple.

The 30th, I dedicated to the memory of the Flight of the Holy Family into Egypt.

The 1st to the 7th day of the following month, I dedicated to honoring the Holy Infant Jesus in His land of exile, worshiping His first steps, His first words,

His first actions, His purity and His simplicity.

The 8th, I dedicated to celebrating the Return of the Holy Family to Nazareth.

The 9th, I dedicated to contemplating Jesus as He began to work with St. Joseph.

The 10th, I dedicated to honoring the obedience which the Child Jesus rendered to the Blessed Virgin and to St. Joseph.

The 11th, I dedicated to ponder on the loving and affectionate attentions which the Child Jesus extended to His Mother, the august guardian of His Sacred Infancy.

The 12th, I dedicated to honoring the Child Jesus at the age of twelve years, when going with Mary and Joseph to Jerusalem, to celebrate the Paschal festivities, He remained in the Temple for three days, concealing Himself from their tender love.

The 13th, I dedicated to worshiping the Holy Child Jesus in the midst of the doctors of the law, upholding the rights of His Divine Father.

The 14th, I dedicated, finally, to adoring the Divine Child Jesus found in the Temple by Mary and Joseph, and returning in their company to Nazareth where He was subject to them.

In this way was ended the month of the Holy Child Jesus, and on the morrow, which was once more the 15th of the month, I would begin again, celebrating the espousals of Mary and Joseph and so on. I experienced such rare happiness in honoring in the above manner the Holy Family on every successive day of the month, that every day was to me like a feast-day. Moreover, the Child Jesus in union with Whom I performed all my actions, made easy and agreeable whatever I undertook to do.

I, therefore, began to look at myself as a house-servant of the Holy Family. I longed also to be invested with the Holy Habit of Carmel, and I asked the Prioress to grant me this grace in spite of my unworthiness. After six months of postulancy, this grace was granted me on May 21, 1840, in the month consecrated to Mary to whom I was indebted for my beautiful vocation.

On that joyous day when I was given the Holy Habit of the Blessed Virgin of Mount Carmel, I dedicated myself to the Holy Family by writing out a special Act of Consecration which I placed over my heart during the ceremony of investiture.

It read as follows:

ACT OF CONSECRATION TO THE HOLY FAMILY

O Jesus, Mary and Joseph, most holy and illustrious family, deign to accept me today in spite of my unworthiness as your servant, for this is the ardent desire of my heart. I resolve to be faithful to you, and while I am not able at this time to bind myself to your service by making the three vows of religion, accept at least my desires so to practice these vows as if in reality I had made them.

O most Holy Infant Jesus, grant me the favor to be ever submissive to the Holy Ghost and to my Superiors, as You were to the Blessed Virgin and to St. Joseph.

And you, Oh, Holy Mary conceived without sin, who are so beautiful and so pure in the eyes of God, obtain for me the grace never to do anything which might tarnish the beautiful virtue of purity.

And you, Oh, blessed Patriarch, St. Joseph, who practiced holy poverty with such consummate perfection, sacrificing yourself for the Holy Infant Jesus and His Mother, deign by your powerful intercession with God that I may follow your example. Grant that I may love and practice holy poverty until the very last breath of my life so that sacrificing myself in labors for my sisters, I may perform these actions as a pleasure rather than a duty.

Finally, as a proof that you accept me this day as your domestic servant, and that my services are agreeable to you, obtain for me the grace to acquit myself worthily of my duties in connection with the Divine Office, so that I may recite it with attention, respect, love, fervor and devotion, being as fully awake at Matins as though I were in heaven, dazzled by the beauty of God and the splendor of His majesty. AMEN.

Ever since this consecration, I have looked upon myself as being a little domestic of the Holy Family, performing all my actions with the intention of serving them at Nazareth. But there was yet one more ambition that I still had, and this ambition was to become, as it were, a little donkey of the Holy Infant Jesus. I felt that if the royal prophet, King David, could regard himself before God as a beast of burden, I could with much more justice qualify for this title. When I reflected that the Son of God had become, for love of us, so poor that in order to make His triumphant entry into Jerusalem, He was constrained to send His disciples to borrow so poor a mount as a donkey, and that they beggingly spoke for Him, saying: "The Master has need of it," I was so moved that I said to our Lord:

"My Saviour, now that You are in heaven, I want You to have on earth, entirely as Your own, a donkey that will always be at Your side to serve You, and one that You can lead wherever You please. Accept me in this role by conferring this title of donkey on me."

As well as I can remember I was so earnestly desirous of learning whether or not our Lord accepted my offer, that I prayed to the Holy Family for this intention. In addition to praying, I also drew up a practical little plan of my own, taking the following steps of procedure to insure having myself accepted in this new role.

It happened that at this time the professed nuns were making their annual retreat, and the postulants and novices therefore spent their recreation in the novitiate. One evening as we were all gathered before a picture of the Holy Family, launching my thought-out plan, I proposed that we should make of our novitiate a sort of Stable of Bethlehem for the Holy Family, each accepting to serve them as a beast of burden according to whatever lot would fall to us. The proposition was accepted unanimously and it was decided that one would be the donkey of the Holy Infant Jesus, another the ox, another the sheep, and so on. We drew lots and to my unbounded satisfaction, Divine Providence allowed me to become the donkey of the Divine Infant Jesus.

I further proceeded to ask for information about the habits of donkeys in order that I might avoid their faults. As one of the postulants, while yet in the world, happened to have owned a donkey, she was well able to give me all the necessary information on this subject. It turned out, we could not have had a more amusing nor a more innocent recreation. Finally we wrote out some tickets to supply information on our particular choice, and mine read as follows:

"The donkey of the Holy Infant Jesus is both hard-headed and lazy. And although this donkey likes only to walk in narrow paths, yet she is resolved to correct herself and her office henceforth shall be to keep the Holy Infant Jesus warm and to bear Him on His various journeys. In short, she is to render every possible service to the Holy Family."

I was charmed with my new title, but in order to make it authentic, I felt I should secure the Prioress' approbation. I, therefore, begged her to sign my ticket, telling myself that since she represented our Lord, obtaining her signature would signify our Lord's acceptance of me under that title. The entire novitiate therefore proceeded to afford our Reverend

Mother an amusing recreation indeed, as we all presented her our tickets. At first she was not too willing to enter into our plan, and to give us her signature, but finally yielding and becoming all things to all, that she might save all, as St. Paul recommends, that is, becoming a child together with her children, she signed our tickets with her initials.

As for myself, I must confess, I had a far-reaching motive in my very serious intention in offering myself to the Holy Infant Jesus for I felt that the signature of the prioress to my little ticket constituted a little contract by which I could proceed to answer that first call of our Lord which He had made me a few days after entering the convent, asking me to make a complete offering of myself to Him, and also to pledge all, even my least merits into His hands for the accomplishment of His special designs.

The truth was that I continually felt myself forcibly drawn to make this act of complete self-abandonment; however, one thing was lacking and that was permission to do so. Now, seeing that our Reverend Mother had signed my little ticket, I began to hope to be able at last to make my little act of sacrifice to the Divine Child Jesus for the accomplishment of His designs. However, to be more sure, I spoke to our Reverend Mother and I asked her if she would consent to give her donkey to the Infant Jesus to do with as He wished. She answered no, instructing me that I should tell this Divine Infant that our Reverend Mother would only lend Him her donkey, but not give it to Him for a while yet.

I was to be refused more than once, for this wise and prudent Mother in her experience could undoubtedly foresee that a perfect Act of Abandonment, such as our Lord desired, for the accomplishment of His special designs, might bring about consequences which my inexperience in the ways of God prevented me from foreseeing. So it was for this reason that the

prioress in her wisdom first submitted me to the tests of
obedience and the renouncing of my will, to make this poor
and miserable instrument more manageable and yielding before
allowing her to be offered to our Lord. I was therefore obliged
to tell the Holy Child Jesus that our Reverend Mother merely
loaned me to Him as His donkey. Presenting myself to Him in
this new role through the hands of Mary and Joseph, I believe
my act of simplicity was agreeable to the Divine Infant for He
began to wield a new power over my soul, directing it in His
ways. This was, indeed, the fulfillment of one of His promises
which He had made me on entering Carmel. I considered my
soul as being the poor stable of Bethlehem, and contemplating
the Holy Infant dwelling in my heart, I adored Him there in
union with Mary and Joseph, offering myself to Him as His
little house-servant. During prayer I considered myself to be
His donkey, warming Him with my love. Then again as I went
through the convent doing such manual work as had been
assigned to me, I imagined myself in the house of Nazareth,
working for the Holy Family.

But the devil who is so proud was, undoubtedly, jealous at
seeing me so taken up with honoring the humiliations of the
Infancy of the Word Incarnate, and one day after I had performed an action which must have proved very displeasing to
him, he tried to revenge himself upon me. That night, after I
had retired and was, I believe, about to fall asleep, I felt
suddenly on my head what seemed like a huge beast wanting
to smother me. Instantly, I experienced an interior warning that
this was the demon. As I felt his claws sink into my head, I
called on the Blessed Virgin with all my strength, asking her to
come to my help, and saw that at the sacred name of Mary, he
took flight. Then I began to pray and as well as I can recall,
I began to sing those adorable words so terrible to the demon,
"And the Word was made flesh and dwelt among us," in spite

of the fact that it was our time of strict silence. Although I did not see him with the eyes of my body, since he crouched himself on top of my head, I was beside myself with fright, for I was inwardly convinced that this was no mere dream, but that it was the demon attempting to smother the donkey of the Divine Infant Jesus, but the Holy Virgin came to its help.

6

My YEAR of novitiate having come to a close, I at once asked our Reverend Mother for the favor of being admitted to Holy Profession of Vows, in spite of my unworthiness. Although she did not seem too anxious, and justifiably so, knowing as she did that I hardly had the proper understanding of what it really meant to become a Carmelite, yet acceding to my entreaties, she made ready for my Profession in spite of my meager virtue and capacity. I was now told that I must present myself three times before the Chapter composed of the Prioress and of the Professed Chapter Sisters in order to ask them to admit me to my Profession of Vows. On learning this, I felt inspired to perform a little exercise of piety each time before presenting myself to the Chapter, to be more sure of securing the Infant Jesus as my spouse. I truly believed that if I hoped to obtain the Divine Infant as my Bridegroom it was necessary for me first to address my petition for this favor to the three persons entitled to exercise any rights over Him, that is, the Eternal Father, the Blessed Virgin and St. Joseph. Having addressed my fervent petitions to these three Persons, I obtained my desired favor, for the community, in spite of my unworthiness, admitted me to make my Profession on June 8, 1841, and thus I celebrated my spiritual nuptials with Jesus, my Divine Spouse.

The priest who, while I was in the world, had directed me in my vocation came to officiate at the ceremony and also preached, taking for his text the words: "All nations shall call Me blessed." Attempting to make me understand the beauty of the state of life which I had embraced, the priest repeated several times in the course of his sermon: "You are blessed." He had good reason for emphasizing this because my vocation was, indeed, replete with delights and full of blessings.

The following is the consecration which I made on this beautiful day.

CONSECRATION

Oh, Eternal God, uniting myself with Jesus, my Saviour, immolated for the salvation of the world, I ask You to accept the full sacrifice of myself which I now make, with Him and through Him.

Oh, Jesus, I offer myself to You on the altar of Your Divine Heart through the hands of Mary and of Joseph, begging them to be the guardians and custodians of my vows.

Oh, dearest Holy Family of my heart, accept the entire donation and consecration which I make of myself to your service. On this day, through the hands of our holy mother St. Teresa, and our holy father St. John of the Cross, I offer myself entirely to You for the accomplishment of your designs in my soul. Look upon me as your property and taking charge of my Holy Vows, fulfill them in me through your powerful protection.

Oh, Jesus, my adorable Spouse, since I am so poor, so miserable and so inconstant in doing good, allow me to borrow all the dispositions and love of your Holy Mother and of her august spouse, for it is through the voice and the heart of Mary and of Joseph that I make my profession, and I promise poverty, chastity and obedience to Almighty God, to our Saviour, and to the Blessed Virgin Mary, under the guidance of our legitimate superiors in accordance with the Primitive Rule of the Order of Mount Carmel, of the Reform of St. Teresa, without any mitigation until death.

Oh, Divine Infant Jesus, on this day I unite my sacrifice to the one which You made to Your Eternal Father at the time of Your Presentation in the Temple. On that occasion You offered Yourself in order to redeem me from my sins, and today I wish to offer myself in turn in order to redeem You from the hands of sinners.

Oh, Mary, my tender Mother and you, my good father St. Joseph, who have offered to the high priests two little doves to repurchase the Infant Jesus, kindly offer to the Eternal Father, upon the Altar of the Heart of Jesus, my body and my soul, to repurchase this Divine Infant from the hands of sinners, and to heal His wounds, particularly those of His Divine Heart which I so desire to love.

Beseech Him, moreover, dear Mary and Joseph, to engrave within my soul all the Features of His Divine Likeness, so that it will not be I any longer who live, but rather that it be Jesus who taking birth again may live in me.

Oh, Jesus, Mary and Joseph, you know with what ardor and joy I would have offered myself as your household servant had I had the blessing of living at the time that you inhabited the earth. It is with these same sentiments of love that I have for you, that I undertake to serve this holy community, and as if I beheld you living in this house, I offer you everything that I will do. As I belong entirely to you, look upon me as your little domestic servant, and dispose of me according to your own pleasure. AMEN.

SISTER MARY OF ST. PETER
AND OF THE HOLY FAMILY,
UNWORTHY CARMELITE

June 8, 1841

Having thus given myself entirely to the Holy Child Jesus

as His little household servant, He very soon inspired me to watch over the flocks of His sheep, grazing on the pasture lands of His Holy Childhood, to which sheep I will refer as the Twelve Tribes of Israel. Our Lord now traced out for me a plan of little spiritual exercises intended to honor the twelve years of His Holy Childhood.

To honor the first year of the Infant Jesus, I offered to Him through the hands of Mary and Joseph the Pope and all ordained clergymen of Holy Church, placing them under the protection of St. Peter and of St. Paul.

To honor the second year of the Infant Jesus, I offered Him all the Religious, placing them under the protection of St. John and the other Holy Apostles.

To honor the third year of the Child Jesus, I offered Him all the Rulers of the earth, placing them under the protection of the Holy King David and the Three Wise Magi-Kings.

To honor the fourth year of the Child Jesus, I offered Him all Freemasons, placing them under the protection of the Holy Martyrs, and asking the Divine Infant for their conversion.

To honor the fifth year of the Child Jesus, I offered Him all Actors, placing them under the protection of St. John the Baptist and of St. Sylvester, in order that the Holy Infant might enlighten them.

To honor the sixth year of the Child Jesus, I offered Him infidel nations, placing them under the protection of the nine choirs of angels, asking them to make the torch of faith shine upon them.

To honor the seventh year of the Child Jesus, I offered Him all heretics and schismatics, placing them under the protection of the Patriarchs.

To honor the eighth year of the Child Jesus, I offered Him the Jews, placing them under the protection of St. Ann and of St. Joachim.

To honor the ninth year of the Child Jesus, I offered Him all unbelievers, placing them under the protection of the holy Prophets.

To honor the tenth year of the Child Jesus, I offered Him all hardened sinners, placing them under the protection of the holy Confessors.

To honor the eleventh year of the Child Jesus, I offered Him all tepid souls, placing them under the protection of the holy Women.

To honor the twelfth year of the Child Jesus, I offered Him all just souls, placing them under the protection of our holy mother St. Teresa and all other Holy Virgins.

Behold then this sheepfold surrounding the crib of the Child Jesus, which I continuously tended, the Saviour in the meantime taking charge of my soul to such a degree that I may well say He was its Director and its Master.

For a very long period I continued to practice the special spiritual exercises honoring the Child Jesus, as I applied myself to meditate exclusively on the mysteries of the Divine Childhood.

But finally our Lord indicated that He wanted me to meditate also on the mysteries of His adult life. He now urged me to honor Him by contemplating daily all the mysteries of His Holy Life. Such a mental exercise which involved meditation on the thirty-three years of the Life of Jesus, to be undertaken and finished in one day, and repeated every day thereafter, might appear complicated. However, although I now practiced it daily, I never found it tiring or fatiguing. All I had to do was to submit to grace and follow the light which our Lord gave me, and thus without any effort on my part I was able to complete these long meditations comprising all the mysteries of the Life of Jesus each day.

When I told our Reverend Mother of these lengthy interior

devotions which I was now inspired to practice, she asked me to give her a full account of them in writing. The following is a copy of the written report which I submitted to her at the time, explaining in detail how I meditated at different hours of the day on the Life of our Saviour.

DAILY MEDITATION

Beginning at eight o'clock in the evening, I offer myself as a little servant to the Blessed Virgin and to St. Joseph, and then I commence to guard and to tend all the nations of the earth, the flocks of the Holy Infant Jesus, which is the Mystical Body and His Holy Wounds, as I adore the Mystery of the Incarnation until nine o'clock.

When the bell announcing Matins rings at nine, I contemplate the birth of the Infant Jesus, uniting myself with the Holy Angels and with the Shepherds and the Magi who adored Him.

At the first Nocturn, I adore the Nativity of the Word in the bosom of His Father, as I contemplate His Divine Life.

At the second Nocturn, I adore His Birth in the stable, as I consider now His mortal life on earth.

At the third Nocturn, I honor His sacramental Birth in the Eucharist, His spiritual Birth in our hearts, and also His glorious life in Heaven after His Ascension.

At the beginning of each of the nine psalms of Matins, I unite myself with the nine choirs of Angels to adore our Lord and Saviour.

At the "Te Deum" which concludes Matins, I adore the Infant Jesus manifesting Himself to the Jews in the persons of the shepherds, who having been invited by the Angels came to adore Him.

Then during the Psalms of Lauds, I adore the Holy Infant circumcised and named Jesus, worshiping Him with the Three

Kings who adored Him as God, as King, and as Man.
Such is my interior occupation during Matins and Lauds.

Returning from these prayers in choir, I enter our cell where I continue further to tend the flocks of the Infant Jesus until eleven o'clock at night. I guard these flocks by begging the Divine Saviour to fill them with blessings, by applying to all these sheep His infinite merits. Finally I go to bed, taking my rest in union with the Holy Infant Jesus as He rests in the manger.

When morning comes, I rise at the first stroke of the bell, and adoring the Eternal Father, I address Him in union with the Infant Jesus saying: "Here I am, my Father. Behold, I come to do Your will."

I then go to the choir for mental prayer, in union with Mary and with Joseph, imagining myself carrying the Holy Infant Jesus to the Temple, and during my prayer I offer myself with Him to His Divine Father. I also renew my Holy Vows. Then I dedicate everything to the Divine Saviour, as I offer Him to the Eternal Father for the salvation of His sheep.

Prayer being finished, I accompany the Holy Family to Nazareth. But soon the bell rings for prayer, this time for the Little Hours of the Holy Office, and I picture myself departing with the Holy Family to Egypt. During the twelve psalms of Prime, Terce, Sext and None, I adore the twelve years of the Holy Child Jesus, honoring His years of exile in Egypt, and concluding with His return to Nazareth, and His discourse in the Temple of Jerusalem in the midst of the doctors of the law.

After Holy Mass, there follow the hours of manual labor, during which time I apply myself to considering the labors and the hidden life of our Lord.

At eleven o'clock, I adore Jesus baptized by St. John, and from noon to one o'clock, I am occupied meditating on Jesus in the desert.

From one to two o'clock, I honor His evangelical life, as I consider His preaching and admonishing.

At two o'clock when the bell rings for Vespers, I adore the triumphant entry of Jesus into Jerusalem and I enter choir in union with Him. During Vespers of the Divine Office, I remain in spirit at His feet, adoring all the sentiments of His Divine Heart during His last week on earth, as I ponder also the excess of His love which constrained Him to institute the Blessed Sacrament of the Altar.

After Vespers I enter in spirit into the Garden of Olives and spend the rest of the late afternoon following our Lord, in union with Mary, as He undergoes the sorrowful passion.

At five o'clock the bell rings for mental prayer. Adoring Jesus crucified, I make my prayer at the foot of the cross, where in the Sacred Heart of Jesus, I begin to examine my conscience. After humbling myself before our Lord for my faults, I give myself entirely to Him, renewing my holy vows in union with the sacrifice of this Divine Saviour on the cross.

After I have in this way given myself anew to our Lord, it seems to me that He reciprocates and in turn gives Himself to me together with all His merits. Uniting my soul with His, He allows me to share all His desires, and to partake of the glory which He renders to His Celestial Father in His Victim State. Thus I lose myself, as with my Divine Spouse I contemplate the glory of God and the salvation of souls. I then find in the Sacred Heart of Jesus all the mysteries of His Holy Life, as I behold there also His merits, and all the flocks of His sheep.

Then I commence to offer the various mysteries of the life of Jesus to the Eternal Father, for this or for another sheepfold of the flocks of the Holy Child Jesus. I proceed also to offer to the Heavenly Father the four parts of the world, placing them in the four sacred wounds of His feet and His hands. I further

[67]

enclose the twelve flocks of sheep of the Holy Family into the Sacred Heart of Jesus.

Next I offer to the Eternal Father the souls in purgatory, placing them in the other wounds of the adorable body of Jesus. Thus do I offer this Holy Victim through the hands of the Blessed Virgin to the Eternal Father as a holocaust in thanksgiving, in expiation, and in petition; and also as a warrant of complacence and of mercy in honor of all the immense perfections of the Most Holy Trinity. Finally, I worship the last sigh of Jesus on the cross. This then is the substance of my meditation with which our Lord inspires me during evening prayer, that is from five to six o'clock.

During the rest of the day I consider Jesus buried in the sepulchre until Complin. Finally I worship Jesus in His glorious resurrection from the tomb, and then I contemplate Him as He ascends into Heaven.

Such are the spiritual exercises which I practice every day. However, in order that our Lord should lead me in this way, it is necessary for me to die to everything that gratifies my senses. For me there remains only one thing and that is to profoundly humble myself. God Alone, His will and His glory, these are my motto. All my actions are governed according to these two quotations from Scripture: "And He was subject to them," as also, "I did not come to be served but to serve."

Our Lord makes me understand very vividly how incapable I am of any good, and how deep is my misery. However, as the Holy Child Jesus leads His donkey with the bridle of His holy grace, I have but to obey Him and renounce myself.

Our Reverend Mother in her wisdom did all she could to ascertain the spirit by which I was led. In order to make me more humble, she used to reprimand and humiliate me, endeavoring to make me proceed along the ordinary road of spiritual perfection. And although I did whatever I could to obey her, yet I soon found myself in the same path. She then made me speak with a priest, well versed in the interior life, a member also of a religious Order, saying to me:

"My child, tell the priest exactly how you make your prayer, and confide to him all that concerns the way God is leading you."

I was grateful to be able to do what our charitable Mother had prescribed, and I opened my soul to this priest. Having examined everything carefully, he said to me:

"My daughter, continue without fear in your present way and allow our Lord to lead you. I assure you that your way of life has a solid foundation for it is grounded on the spirit of self-denial. Tell your Reverend Mother that I am satisfied, and that I will also speak with her."

Our prudent Mother thereupon permitted me to abandon myself to the spirit of God, and she even gave me a wise counsel, urging me to be very faithful to His inspirations of grace. She told me however to respond to the call of grace only when I was drawn by it, and to return to active works when the operation of God had passed. But since I had no employment to distract me from feeling the presence of God, all my days were but one endless meditation, if I may so express myself. What work I did have did not prevent me in the least from continually communing with our Lord. Since I was not tried by distractions or dryness, I suppose I did not gain much merit.

However, very soon our charitable Mother, who watched zealously over my soul and my spiritual progress, entrusted me with an occupation well intended to force me to practice self-denial. The office which she now gave me was that of Portress.

This employment, so distracting, was not at all in harmony

with my attraction for prayer and for silence. But I looked upon this order of our Reverend Mother as a command from heaven and I submitted to it with joy. Reflecting moreover that I was given this office on Christmas Day itself, I deemed this as a sure sign that the Holy Infant Jesus had chosen me to be His little household servant and that He intended from now on to employ me as such by allowing me to run the errands in His house. I then made a new offering of myself to the Divine Child.

Assuming my new duties I wished very much to have a small statue of the Divine Child in order to give Him more homage. Not daring, however, to ask Reverend Mother for one, it seemed to me one day that this Divine Infant told me me that I had but to ask for it and that it would be given to me. I did as I was urged and the favor was granted me. So it was that I now had a statue of the Holy Infant Jesus while at work in our turn-room, where I offered Him all my little labors, asking Him to give me souls as payment for my errands. In spite of my unworthiness this Divine Child supplied all the graces I needed for my new work as portress in such a way that it in no way prevented my interior recollection, nor did it keep me from being united to our Lord at prayer time. I used to weep during the day for the salvation of the flocks of sheep of the Holy Child Jesus and at prayer in the evening He would repay me a hundredfold.

But since at certain times during the day, through a powerful grace, I would feel our Lord's presence sensibly in my soul, I used to leave off doing some of my work for a short while in order to harken to His voice with greater ease. One day as I wondered whether this was allowed without first securing permission, I went to the Reverend Mother asking for it. Since her solicitude for my soul was such that she overlooked nothing that would help me practice self-denial, she forbade me to stop work to heed these interior communications of grace, adding:

"However, I do permit you to rest a bit when you feel yourself very much distracted."

Thanks be to God, I followed all her wise counsels feeling that she showed much charity towards my soul, and realizing too that she had a special grace to lead me.

I think it was in 1843, that our Lord told me to pray in a very particular manner for Spain which was at that time ravaged by a revolution. I have never before felt my soul so united to our Lord as I did during this time, as I saw Him accomplishing in me something which I can neither explain nor understand. It seems to me that I heard our Lord asking special graces for Spain from His Eternal Father, and in so pressing a manner, that I was very much astonished. It seemed to me, too, that He invited me to plead for this cause in His name. As I commence to explain this deep mystery of love, I see that instead of clarifying it, I only make it appear more involved, and therefore I prefer to abandon it, leaving it to God.

7

As TIME went on, I still felt myself interiorly very much pressed by our Lord to make that Act of complete abandonment of myself for the accomplishment of His designs. However, as yet I had not succeeded in obtaining my superior's permission to make this Act. In 1843, however, Providence presented me with an opportunity to reiterate my petition for this favor. The case was as follows:

There was question of our leaving the old convent and trying to find a good location for a new monastery. Reverend Mother, being deeply concerned over the project, asked me to pray to the Holy Infant Jesus and ask Him to give us a suitable piece of ground on which to build our new convent. Praying, I asked for this favor as I was told to do, but the Divine Child answered me in the center of my heart, saying: "Give me first the ground of your soul!"

I understood perfectly what our Divine Saviour meant. He, too, had in mind the construction of a certain edifice which He wished to build to the glory of His Eternal Father, and He had a long time ago chosen the poor ground of my soul for this project so that His designs might be accomplished, in spite of my unworthiness. The fact that He should choose so miserable an instrument as myself was meant to redound finally to His own greater glory.

I now went in search of Reverend Mother and finding her I soon learned from the many things she told me that she was depressed with many worries over the new building project being contemplated. Seeing her anxiety, I felt that she could stand a bit of recreation and therefore I attempted to amuse her with a bit of humorous conversation which soon made her laugh heartily.

"Reverend Mother," I said to her, "when people find themselves without any money in their house, and wish to raise some in a hurry, do you know what they do? Why, they sell their beast of burden. And therefore, I am convinced that if you would decide to sell me to the Holy Infant Jesus He would pay you so well that you would have enough money to build your monastery."

Although Reverend Mother seemed very amused at my proposal, I would not allow her to laugh it off merely so I insisted:

"Look, Mother, I know I am not worth much, but since the Holy Infant Jesus wants me, and since He asks for me, He will most certainly pay the purchase price."

I was simply charmed by the idea of being able to sell myself for our Lord who, I reflected, for love of me had allowed Himself to be sold by Judas, and therefore I pressed Reverend Mother as follows:

"Mother, what price will you ask for me?"

The prioress hearing me speak so earnestly on this matter, began no doubt to realize that our Lord might have some designs in inspiring me so deeply to make this unusual petition. Assuming an attitude of seriousness, she now answered:

"Very well, my child, go and tell the Divine Infant that if I were rich, I would give you to Him outright. But since I am poor and am presently in great need of money in order to build His holy house, I find myself obliged to sell you. Ask Him, therefore, to purchase you."

This reply gave me a great deal of pleasure. Addressing

myself prayerfully to the Holy Child Jesus, I gave him Reverend Mother's message and begged Him to purchase me in order that I might become entirely His property according to His will.

One night shortly thereafter, while I was at prayer warmly presenting Him with the love of the shepherds, the magi and other saints who had seen and adored Him in life, I wove for Him, through my meditations, a garland in honor of the twelve years of His Holy Childhood. I believe this little devotion was very pleasing to Him because I think I saw Him in the center of my soul, and He spoke to me words similar to the following:

"Tell your Mother Prioress to write a letter to a certain person, and she will receive from her an alms towards the building of the new convent."

What joyous news! Already I felt that here was proof that the Holy Child seemed willing to purchase His little donkey. I ran to our good Mother to acquaint her with these developments. The person whom the Divine Infant had named to me lived about sixty leagues from Tours and I was only slightly acquainted with her, whereas Reverend Mother did not know her at all.

To test somewhat the genuineness of this communication which I reported to her, the prioress wrote to that person, however, saying nothing at all in her letter of the manner in which the Infant Jesus indicated to me that she write. As an answer was somewhat slow in arriving, I began to doubt a little but the Holy Child reassured me. Finally a letter came from this lady, and with it was enclosed a donation of 500 francs towards the building of our new convent.

This was one of the first contributions that the Mother Prioress received and it seemed like a deposit on what this Divine Saviour intended to give her in the future. I was filled with joy when this alms arrived and I said the "Laudate" five hundred times in thanksgiving to honor the Divine Child.

Next I went to the prioress suggesting that since five hundred francs was more than sufficient to buy a donkey, would she consent now that the Child Jesus had sent her this sum to turn me over completely to Him as His own property? She, however, still desiring to try my patience and to test my spirit made me understand that she needed much more money than what had been received to build the house of our Lord, after which she would give me permission to deliver myself to the Holy Child Jesus for the accomplishment of His designs.

I, therefore, returned once more and fervently begged Him to help Reverend Mother in the huge project that faced her.

One day after this during prayertime it seemed to me that I found myself as it were in the center of a building project. Our Lord then made me understand how glorious a thing it really is and also how meritorious to build Him a house. He further made me comprehend that the prioress would have many worries in the course of the construction project, but He told me that I would furnish her with the stones necessary to build the house.

He also told me to inform the prioress not to fret over money saying that if the house were built according to the spirit of our mother St. Teresa, He Himself would pay for everything and that we would have donations arriving to us from all sides.

"But," He added, "if, on the contrary, the house is not built according to this spirit, let pay whoever will!"

I found myself deeply embarrassed to be forced to deliver this message to Reverend Mother. In fact, I hardly dared approach her with it, but at last, doing violence to myself, I went to her in order to carry out the will of our Lord. When I finished telling the prioress what our Lord had made me hear, she confessed to me that all during the previous night she had hardly slept at all because she was very much worried over the building plan which the architect had just submitted to her, since this blueprint was not at all suitable for a Carmelite foundation.

She, therefore, set about at once to have an entirely different set of plans drawn, so that the new monastery would be in conformity with the spirit of our mother St. Teresa. After this, our Lord well pleased with the building project now indicated that He was ready to fulfill His part of the promise. As for the stones which I was to furnish for the building of our Lord's house, they were to be purchased with a good deal of trouble, for as our Lord later made known to me, these stones were the Prayers of Reparation to the Holy Face, to atone for blasphemies against the Holy Name of God, which prayers were destined to bring down on our cloister great blessings.

The moment was approaching for God to accomplish His designs in my soul, for one day while I was opening my heart to Reverend Mother and telling her of the extraordinary communications and favors which I had the grace of receiving from our Lord, in spite of my unworthiness, during those years before entering the convent, she told me that, perhaps I had since proved myself somewhat unfaithful to God, since these unusual favors had ceased, and for me now to make atonement. She urged me to pray that our Saviour would place my soul in the same dispositions which I had in the past when our Lord favored me with those exalted communications. I obeyed.

Shortly afterwards our Lord invited me to apply myself particularly to honoring His Divine Heart and also the Heart of His holy Mother, promising me that He would favor me in the future with graces even more extraordinary than those which He had in the past conferred upon me.

I did what our Lord assigned to me, and honoring the Heart of Jesus and the Heart of Mary, I applied myself with great devotion to these two hearts. However, before granting me further graces our Lord prepared my soul now by plunging it into great interior sufferings. I began to experience during prayer a loving and a burning attraction to the Three Persons of the Most Blessed Trinity. Feeling myself constrained repeatedly to renew my vows, I henceforth dedicated the three powers of my soul to the Three adorable Persons in God, Who now operated great marvels in my soul, but in a manner which I am unable to explain. I was plunged in an abyss of suffering born as it were of my immense desire to glorify God, but recognizing my extreme misery, I felt annihilated and incapable of anything good.

Finally, our Lord having purified my soul according to His designs, in spite of my unworthiness, communicated Himself to me on August 26, 1843, speaking to me for the first time about His great Work of the Reparation for blasphemy, destined to redound to the glory of the Holy Name of God. However, since I have written about this elsewhere, I will not here speak of it in detail.

I will mention merely that I received from our Lord several communications on the subject of this Work, of which I have rendered an exact account to my superiors, who in their wisdom and prudence soon forbade me to occupy myself with it. I was even forbidden to think about it. Furthermore, when I submitted an account of the prayers of reparation to the glory of the Holy Name of God which it pleased our Lord to make known to me, our Reverend Mother took these prayers away from me and would not permit me to recite them. Since I was persuaded that my superiors would do nothing except through God's Providence, I submitted to their orders and did everything in my power to obey them.

But our Lord, if I may so express myself, made a hole for me in the wall of obedience, by coming into my heart, or rather drawing me entirely to Himself in order to speak further to me about His Work. One day, while visiting our Reverend Mother to give her an account of my interior dispositions, I told her that in my prayer I was continually drawn to make Reparation for the outrages committed against God by blasphemers. She scolded me very much and forbade me to continue these prayers. Ordering me to apply myself to a simple consideration of my last end, or some other subject, she said that instead of occupying myself in trying to make reparation for others, it would be better if I prayed for myself, for perhaps I had blasphemed God in my own heart: "Why do you not meditate on words which God may some day say to you, such as 'Go ye accursed into everlasting fire'?"

Now, deeply afflicted at seeing Reverend Mother so displeased with me I turned to our Lord for help for, indeed, I had a great fear of disobeying the orders of my superior and, on the other hand, I did not know how to set about changing my method of prayer by going contrary to the light which our Lord placed in my soul. So applying myself rigidly to meditate on the subject which the Prioress indicated, I later went to give her an account of my meditation asking her to tell me whether I had fulfilled her command. When Reverend Mother assured me that I did well, I found calm restored within my soul. After that our Lord one day made me understand that I must obey my superiors rather than any communication which I believed that He Himself had given me.

Nevertheless, in the midst of all this, my soul was in fearful straits for I found no consolation anywhere, neither in my confessor nor in my superiors who in their wisdom wanted to test my spirit in order to assure themselves whether, indeed, this was the work of God. Then it was that I felt the crushing weight of that Cross which our Lord had promised He would give me after I became a Religious, which promise had been made to me long before I entered Carmel.

So it happened that whenever our Lord would communicate to me anything on the subject of His Work of Reparation, I did not dare to speak of it to our good Mother, but writing everything down, I would bring my account to her in her office, glad indeed, whenever I found that she was not there. I remember trembling from head to toes, holding the little letter I had written in my hand, and standing with it before the Blessed Sacrament to offer it to Him there before daring to bring it to the prioress.

This Work was at times like a devouring flame within me. While my whole being longed to speak of the Work of Reparation to someone who might be interested, I was forbidden to say a word about it. Finally, one day our Lord granted me an unusual consolation. I was giving Reverend Mother an account of my interior sufferings and telling her how much the Work of Reparation entrusted to me had cost me in anguish. Our good Mother then said to me:

"My child, what do you want of me? I can do nothing for you. You must give birth to this Work in pain."

Suddenly, through an act of Providence something fell from the book which Reverend Mother just then held in her hands. It was a small picture on which was also printed an Act of Reparation to the Most Holy Name of God, followed by an urgent warning to the people of France to make an effort to appease the anger of God aroused because of blasphemies. In fact, everything which was printed on this notice had a most striking resemblance to all the communications which I had received from our Lord on the topic of Reparation.

Reverend Mother was greatly astonished for she never even knew of the existence of this pamphlet until now. As for me,

I was ravished with joy for certainly here was a sign that our Lord came to my rescue by permitting this incident of the printed prayer to come to light at the very moment that I was opening my soul to our good Mother telling her about the anguish I endured in connection with being charged to promote this Work of Reparation, all of which still seemed to her but a chimera of my imagination.

Examining the pamphlet, Reverend Mother noted that it had been printed in 1819 by Monsignor Soyer, at that time the Vicar General of Poitiers, and later the Bishop of Lucon. The pamphlet was entitled *Warning to the People of France.* Under a sub-title, "Reparation will appease the anger of God," the pamphlet went on to explain that blasphemies were rampant and that they were drawing down the anger of God, all of which was exactly what our Lord had been telling me.

Turning to me with a smile, our good Mother now said to me somewhat amused:

"Sister, if I did not know you as well as I do, I might take you to be a sorceress," to which I replied:

"Reverend Mother, it is the Holy Angels who have placed this pamphlet in your hands."

I was quite sure of this for I had invoked them before coming to speak with the prioress, and undoubtedly the Holy Angels came to my assistance by making this particular book come into notice at the moment. It turned out too that not only was Reverend Mother and I completely unacquainted with the existence of the pamphlet in question, but none of the sisters in the house had ever known of it until then.

Pushing the matter to a final conclusion, Reverend Mother wrote to the Bishop of Lucon who had published that pamphlet in 1819, asking him for some information on the subject. He answered her saying that it was he who had published that pamphlet at the request of a very chosen soul, a Carmelite of

Poitiers, with whom our Lord communed very intimately, and who was certainly led in extraordinary ways. "This wonderful Carmelite," wrote Bishop Soyer, "was a most mortified soul, as also the most humble and the most holy that I have ever known. For the edification of your Order, her life should be written."

This admirable Carmelite whose name was Mother Adelaide had died July 31, 1843, and it was only twenty-six days after her death, that is on August 26, 1843, that our Lord chose me to inherit this, His Work of Reparation, by speaking of it to me for the first time. But alas, if our Lord had bequeathed to me her Work, I recognized now how great a need there was for me also to inherit her virtues, for I felt very much devoid of them.

At this time, also, our Lord permitted that my superiors should learn that Pope Gregory XVI had just granted, on August 8, 1843, a Brief, authorizing a Confraternity of Reparation for blasphemy in Rome, under the patronage of St. Louis, King of France. I felt that the knowledge of this concurring event would serve as convincing proof for my superiors to determine the spirit which led me.

However, when my superiors examined the rules of this Confraternity of Reparation already in existence at Rome, questioning the need of another similar Confraternity, for which I begged, our Lord told me to explain to them that His Work of Reparation revealed to me was to have as its aim not only reparation for blasphemy, but also reparation for the profanation of the Holy Day of the Lord, both enormous sins, arousing the anger of God.

Besides it seems noteworthy to mention here that the particular date of August 26, 1843, on which our Lord spoke to me for the first time on the subject of reparation, had also a special significance in the light of the following incident. In

several parishes of the city of Tours, a very pious gentleman*
had distributed a leaflet containing a prayer, honoring the Holy
Name of God, and imploring, through the intercession of St.
Louis, the extirpation of blasphemy. This novena of prayers
had been made for nine days preceding August 25, the Feast
of St. Louis. What is remarkable in connection with this
novena leaflet is that whereas it had been circulated in parishes
throughout the city, as we later found out, none of these
pamphlets reached our Carmel. Then on the day after the
Feast of St. Louis, that is on August 26, our Lord communicated
to me, the most unworthy of the community of Carmelites,
the fruit of the prayers of these pious souls.

All these strokes of Providence gathered together tended
to enlighten my worthy superiors as to the operations of God
in my soul. In consequence of this I was now permitted to
occupy myself with the Work of Reparation according to the
inspirations which our Lord would give me. Reverend Mother
also returned to me the Prayers of Reparation which our Lord
had inspired me to write down, and I was ravished with joy
at this, for having my Prayers back again, I now began to recite
them every day with much fervor.

Our Lord then made known to me that these prayers were
very agreeable to Him. Finally, one day, He told me that I
must ask my superiors to have these prayers printed. From
this communication there now came to me a new source of
trouble, for our wise prioress, seeing that our Lord continued
to press for His Work in my soul, desired to establish it on a
sure foundation in order to determine still further whether it
was truly the spirit of God that led me.

One day she told me that I appeared to her as another
Pierre Michel. This man was a visionary who had fooled quite

---

* Leo Dupont, in *God Demands Reparation*, edited by Rev. Emeric B. Scallan,
S.T.B. (1952, The William-Frederick Press, New York).

a number of people with his false reports about his revelations. Although he had also paid a visit to our Reverend Mother, she was not at all taken in by his false trickery, for she recognized at once by what spirit he was led. Apprehended later, this man was condemned to several years' imprisonment. Seeing myself actually compared with such an individual, I hardly knew what to think of my communications.

Then one day our Lord reassured me, saying: "As long as you are obedient and humble, and nourish no bitterness in your heart, you can rest assured that you are not being deceived."

Soon after this, Reverend Mother became very ill. I loved her very much and had great confidence in her, although she often scolded me for the good of my soul and to make sure of the work of God within me.

One day during prayer, our Lord told me that to obtain the cure of our Reverend Mother, the community must, for nine days, recite the Prayers of Reparation which I had composed. Our Lord also mentioned that we should add a few acts of mortification, and that if this were done, the prioress would soon be able to resume her duties in the convent.

I made all this known to our dear sick Mother, and begged her to allow the community to make this novena for her cure. She consented to this, but since none of the sisters knew that it was I who had been inspired to compose these prayers, and since they would readily recognize my handwriting were I to pen them, to prevent them from even suspecting my part in this, it was decided that our confessor should copy these prayers. Therefore, it was believed by the sisters that this new devotion came from him. The community made this novena and our Lord fulfilled His promise. Our Reverend Mother was soon well enough to be able to attend to her regular work.

In all this, our Lord was showing my superiors, if I can so

express myself, that He had chosen the ground of my soul, planning to build upon it a certain edifice. I refer to the Work of Reparation. For it was easy by now to see that it was for the accomplishment of His designs in this same Work that He had invited me to offer Him an Act of Perfect Abandonment of myself from the time I first entered Religion, of which I have already spoken many times, and which my superiors in their prudence had judged proper to refuse me to make.

BUT NOW the hour had come and our Lord indicated that He would not proceed to construct His edifice on the ground of my soul without this special Act. On the eve of the renewal of my holy vows, it seems to me that I saw the Holy Child Jesus intimately in my soul, and I begged Him to take entire possession of my being that nothing might remain in me that would not belong to Him. But so that He could accomplish His designs within me, it now seemed to me that He desired and asked me again for a Complete Act of Perfect Oblation.

True, I had already made Him a small Act of self-abandonment in writing which I showed to Reverend Mother, asking her to permit me to make it, which she did, but it was to be only a simple, ordinary act of consecration. Now the Divine Child made me understand that I had received permission to make that act only very imperfectly, and that I had been somewhat remiss since I had not explained myself fully as to the nature of this oblation to my superior. Hence, the Holy Infant Jesus made me understand that if I really wanted my soul to belong entirely to Him, in order that He could operate all that He wished within me, it was absolutely necessary for me to ask again and to obtain the full and explicit consent of my superiors to make this Perfect Act of Self-Sacrifice.

This fault for which the Holy Infant now reproached me, although He accepted it in good faith, I must here confess. This is the way it happened. It has undoubtedly been noticed by now that on several occasions I had asked permission to make the Act of Perfect Abandonment which the Lord demanded of me for the accomplishment of His designs, but always it was judged proper not to allow me to make this Act. Offering my will to our Lord I always submitted to obedience. But one day on the Feast of the Annunciation, I experienced a fervent overflow of Devotion towards the Divine Child Jesus, and learning that one of the sisters in our convent also experienced a similar attraction to the Holy Infancy of our Lord, we both agreed to consecrate ourselves in a special manner to this Divine Child, it being March 25, the Feast of His Incarnation.

I was given the task of composing the Act of Consecration, and I proceeded to formulate this prayer in such a way that it might answer as the perfect donation of myself for which our Lord so repeatedly asked me. Not wishing to make this Act without permission, however, yet fearing that I would again be refused were I to ask it myself, I induced the other sister to ask Reverend Mother's permission for both of us to make this Act and our good Mother allowed us to do it. I was filled with joy thinking within myself that I had at last attained to my goal.

But I soon learned that the Divine Infant Jesus does not like guile, and that He received this Act from me merely as a simple act of consecration, which was the intention of my superioress when she granted her permission.

In consequence of this, the Divine Child now told me that I must expressly ask for this permission from my superiors anew, in order to receive from them their full consent. Very humbly, therefore, I confessed my fault to our Reverend Mother, and explained to her what our Lord had me understand. She in turn took it up with our confessor, and finally, by the Grace of God, I was given full permission to make my Act of Perfect Self-Sacrifice.

It seems important for me to mention here how altogether right it was that our Lord should expressly demand an Act of complete self-abandonment of myself for the accomplishment of His designs, in view of the fact that He is the Sovereign Master of all His creatures? Should He therefore not be free to do in their persons and in them all that He wants?

As for our Lord desiring me to secure first the consent of my superiors before making my Act of Oblation, this was essential since they were to have a large share in the Work which the Divine Saviour wanted to build on the poor ground of my soul. I was to be of service to them only as a puny instrument employed in this project of God, and since they were to suffer many contradictions in the Work of Reparation, our Lord respected, in a way, their free will.

I made the following Act of Oblation on December 25, 1843, the Feast of the Birth of the Holy Infant Jesus. I placed the written formula in the hands of the Blessed Virgin just before Matins of the Feast of Christmas, begging her to offer this Act to Jesus born at midnight in the stable at Bethlehem.

ACT OF PERFECT OBLATION TO THE MOST HOLY CHILD JESUS, ACCORDING TO HIS WILL IN MY REGARD, FOR THE ACCOMPLISHMENT OF HIS DESIGNS TO THE GLORY OF THE HOLY NAME OF GOD

Oh, Most Holy and most amiable Child Jesus, behold the day which I have so much desired has at last arrived. Now, without fear of failing in obedience, I can with all freedom offer myself entirely to You for the accomplishment of Your designs, to whatever extent You may desire to exercise Your will and Your power over my soul.

I am very unworthy, it is true, to make You this offering, but Oh, Divine Child, since it seems to me that You desire this, deign to purify me, Your victim, by the tears of Your Holy Infancy and by Your Most Precious Blood.

Yes, on this ever memorable night of Your august birth, my Divine Spouse, bending low before You in Your crib, I freely offer my entire being to You, through the blessed hands of Mary and of Joseph on the altar of Your heart inflamed with love, and it is there that under the protection of the angels and the saints, I make You an act of entire abandonment of myself, and I resign to You also whatever meager merits I have acquired since the day of my birth, and also of all those merits which I may acquire until the day of my death through Your holy grace, all for the accomplishment of Your designs and for the glory of the Holy Name of God.

Oh, Divine Child, You Who did say to Your holy mother when she found You in the temple of Jerusalem: "Why did you seek me? Did you not know that I must be about My Father's business?" deign to receive me as Your disciple. Grant that from now on, I may, in union with You, be occupied only with those things that appertain to the service of Your Eternal Father, for the glory of His Holy Name.

Oh, most Holy Child, God and man, I renounce myself, and I give myself entirely to You. Do with me and in me all that will please You for the accomplishment of Your designs. I am Your property, therefore take possession of me completely. Yes, Oh, Divine Child, with all my heart and most affectionately for Your sake do I divest myself of everything to the end of my life. Deign, therefore, in Your great mercy, to clothe me with the robe of Your sacred merits which is perfumed with the sweet odor of Your virtues, so that on the day of judgment, I may receive the blessing of Your Heavenly Father.

I take as notary of this contract made with the Holy Child

Jesus, our blessed father, Peter of Berulle, Apostle of the Incarnate Word, and for witnesses and protectors I take all the angels and saints of Heaven.

SISTER MARY OF ST. PETER
AND OF THE HOLY FAMILY,
UNWORTHY CARMELITE

This Act was made at Midnight, December 25, Christmas of the year 1843.

Having made this Act to our Lord, in spite of my unworthiness, He now regarded me entirely as His own, and He went on to build in my soul His edifice to the glory of the Holy Name of God. Since I have written elsewhere of the various communications of our Lord on this subject of Reparation, I will not speak about this Work here. I will only mention in passing that our Lord now began pressing me ever more urgently to ask my superiors to propagate the devotion by having the prayers of Reparation printed in order that they might redound to the glory of God's Holy Name.

But when I addressed this petition to Reverend Mother, she scolded me severely, saying that it was outright presumption on my part to come and ask her to publish prayers which I myself had composed. She further reproved me, saying that it would be much more proper and better for me to recite the beautiful prayers which were composed by the holy Fathers, but that I, being persistently stubborn, chose always to think only about this Work of Reparation. Enduring all these disappointments, I offered them to the Blessed Virgin as money of a spiritual nature in order that with it she could pay for the printing of the leaflets containing the prayers which her Divine Son willed should be distributed throughout the world.

In the meantime, our Saviour began to grant great favors to the Sisters of our Community, who started to recite these prayers of reparation, either for themselves or for their relatives. Since they were altogether ignorant as to who was the author of those prayers, they spoke about them freely in my presence, saying: "Truly, we obtain everything we want from our Lord, merely by making the Novena of Reparation."

About this time, one of our Sisters who was very sick felt herself very much drawn to promise our Lord that she would make a Novena of Reparation for her cure. On the third day of her Novena she felt herself suddenly cured. When she told me about this, I was very happy to learn that our Lord was granting some remarkable favors through the Prayers of Reparation, for this confirmed my belief that I was not being deceived, and that the communications which I had received through God's grace, concerning this Work, were not illusions.

Then one day after Holy Communion, our Lord Himself wishing to console me, in spite of my unworthiness, spoke to me these words, which were later fulfilled: "My daughter, these prayers of reparation will be printed and they will be spread!"

At this period, my superiors, ever charitable, entered into very serious deliberations, to re-examine the operations in my soul to be assured that it was really God's spirit that was leading me. The result was that they ordered me to give them now an account in writing of all my interior dispositions. The following is the report I then drew up for them:

My Reverend and most honored Mother, with the help of the Divine Child Jesus and my Guardian Angel, I shall endeavor to fulfill the order which you have given me, and I will here render an account to you of the manner in which I make my prayer. This is somewhat difficult for me to do, but obedience will help me, and since you are accustomed to my meager capacity of expression, you will be enabled to recognize what are my interior dispositions, and that alone is what matters.

In the first place, I must say that I have no merit whatever in my prayers because praying comes naturally to my soul. This gift of God has been mine since early childhood, despite my unworthiness. As a remote preparation for prayer, I try not to lose sight of our Lord, and this I achieve interiorly by keeping Him company the whole day long. Leaving to the Divine Saviour the charge and care of my relatives and all that concerns my needs, I look at myself as the house-servant of the Holy Family. Therefore, everything that I do in fulfilling the office of portress I consider as if it were actually done by me in the little house of Nazareth. I proceed each day to attend to the three special duties of any servant, which in my opinion are, first, to be ever near the master, second to execute all his orders, and third to look after his interests, by guarding the flocks on his estate, fulfilling all duties strictly in accordance with the master's will.

This then is what I try to do, by the grace of God. Interiorly, I accompany our Lord by meditating on the mysteries of His life as I unite with Him to render praises to God. Secondly, I attend to His errands, considering His words in the Gospel: "And He was subject to them," so that each time the bell at the turn calls me to duty, I offer myself as a sacrifice to the Eternal Father, on the Altar of the Sacred Heart of Jesus, begging Him to unite me with His Divine Son so that it may be Jesus Himself who acts in me.

When I have no distracting occupations, I converse with our Lord. I lead His flocks to pasture, that is, I meditate on His Mysteries, and His merits which serve as food for our souls. I also pray for the bishops of the Church and for the conversion of sinners and I try to avoid distractions, uniting all my actions to those of the Divine Saviour. As a result, exterior occupations hardly ever distract my soul but rather they tend to increase my longing for the repose of prayer. Then when the hour prescribed for this spiritual exercise arrives, our Lord repays me for my little sacrifices of the day.

At the beginning of prayer I make an examination of conscience after which I humble myself at the feet of our Lord for my infidelities as I beg Him mercifully to purify my soul. After that I treat the Saviour with much simplicity, as a child would treat its father. The following is one method of prayer which our Lord one day gave me, although I cannot say whether He did this by speaking His interior words to me or merely by giving me an illumination:

Empty your soul by recollection,
Purify it by an act of contrition,
Then fill it with God.

But since it is useless to continue pouring into a vase once it is filled, so also is it useless to load the soul with new acts and new thoughts when One alone fills and occupies it.

Then again at certain times I feel myelf interiorly carried away with the desire of making the "prayer of union" with our Lord, as He offers Himself to His Celestial Father for His glory and for the salvation of souls. At such times I soon find myself recollected in the Sacred Heart of Jesus. Then as I continue to ponder this Great Sacrifice, I find ample material for meditation. Thus, finding myself clothed with our Lord Jesus Christ, I am more readily able to approach His Celestial Father. Seeing myself enriched by His merits, I no longer fear to ask God for great graces for Holy Church and for the salvation of many souls, since in this union of my soul with Jesus it seems to me that He gives me all His merits that I might offer them to His Father.

I often yield to this kind of prayer, which is not entirely supernatural, except that I do feel that the faculties of my soul are gathered in the Sacred Heart and thus our Lord acts in me and I in Him. At such times, distractions are rare because the imagination is held captive.

However, when I am in this state, close to our Lord, and He desires to communicate something to me on the subject of His Work of Reparation, He then proceeds to work in my soul a second operation. At such times I feel that I myself am powerless to form any interior acts. It appears to me that my own mind is emptied of everything in order to make room for that of our Lord, and it is while I am in this state that my soul listens to His interior words. The more perfect this annihilation becomes, the happier is my soul. At such times it appears as if the soul were melted in God. In this state it discovers itself lost in God without knowing how it entered there. In short, a dominant attraction of grace seizes the soul, raises it above itself, and plunges it into God. Oh, what delightful moments! But this state of perfect contemplation I experience only rarely. It is an altogether gratuitous favor from God and I am altogether unworthy of such a great grace.

My usual method then is to make my prayer in the Sacred Heart of Jesus, where He discloses to me His will, allows me to share His desires of glorifying the Eternal Father and of laboring for the salvation of souls. In praying thus I find much happiness.

As for discursive meditations, I am never able to make these over a long period of time, first because I have no ability for this, and second because my soul is so quickly attracted to our Lord by a movement that springs towards me from His Sacred Heart, that I find myself rapidly enshrined in this divine sanctuary, as a little child might find itself folded in the bosom of its mother.

It is then that my will and my affections do everything while my poor mind is relieved from working. It is our Lord Himself Who has called me to this kind of prayer. In the beginning I did not dare to follow this inclination, fearing that by yielding to it I would fail to make my methodical meditation. Then our Lord, desiring me to follow His will, suggested to me the following comparison: "If the king were to invite you to dinner, would it not be ridiculous for you to bring your dinner along with you, when you could be feasted with food from the host's table to which you had been invited?"

Having sought counsel as to this method of prayer, I was told not to fear, but to follow in the way opened for me by the Holy Spirit, which method was the best. I have since experienced its blessings. I find, indeed, that the banquets of the Sacred Heart of Jesus surpass all those prepared by dint of my human mental exertions. So it happens often that the hour prescribed for prayer comes to an end before I have had time to offer thanks to my Benefactor for these delicious repasts. Hastening then to make a brief act of thanksgiving, I resolve never to lose sight of the One who had the charity to treat me with such generosity, in spite of my unworthiness, promising to serve Him more faithfully in the future.

Notwithstanding all this, I am not without experiencing also from time to time a complete absence of all consolations, but then aridity and interior sufferings are at times very necessary for the soul. Therefore, I accept whatever nourishment our Lord sees fit to give me.

9

Now ARRIVED the hour when I was to endure a very great trial which our Lord had reserved for me. We were obliged to leave the convent so dear to me, where I made my Vows, and where I received so many graces from our Lord's Divine and merciful liberality and to move into a secular house with no enclosure grating. Since I still held the office of portress, my duties brought me in close contact with all sorts of people.

Realizing that it would be at least two years before the new convent would be completed, I saw myself confined to this parlor without any grating. Noticing in the meantime what a large number of persons were coming, all of whom asked to speak to us, some to recommend their sick, others to ask for prayers for the conversion of sinners in whom they were interested, and again others to be consoled in their troubles, and some only from idle curiosity, alas, all this plunged me into real pain.

I began to fear that in such surroundings I might lose the spirit of silence and recollection for which I felt a strong attraction. I wondered, too, if I would ever again be able to hear the voice of my Saviour in such a place. Seeking out the Prioress, I told her of my extreme repugnance for the position of portress in a house without enclosure gratings. Of course, I felt quite certain that on hearing me out she would relieve me from this employment which had become so painful to me, or that she would at least have the kindness to give me a companion who would share the parlor duties with me since this work was so distracting.

But Reverend Mother, notwithstanding her great charity, judged it proper that I should continue to discharge all the duties in the office of portress without an assistant. Only later did she reveal to me that her reason for leaving me at the turn alone at that time was to try me, in order to be better convinced as to the genuineness of my communications on the Work of Reparation.

I wish to mention here for the greater glory of God that, indeed, were the Work of Reparation merely a phantom of my imagination, it would have disappeared in the midst of the distracting trials to which I became continually exposed in my new situation as turn-sister in a secular house without proper enclosure. As a result of being incessantly disturbed by various people who came to tell me all their troubles, I should have forgotten completely about the Work of the Reparation.

To reduce the large number of frequent parlor calls, I tried to explain to the visitors that the real work of a Carmelite nun was to speak much to God in solitude and only very little to people. I also suggested to them to go to other religious houses, that were not bound by such strict rules of silence and retreat as were Carmelites, and to seek consolation there, and that we on our part would pray for their intentions. But all my arguments proved altogether useless. I cannot help laughing even now when I recall a good woman who insisted on bringing her daughter to me in order that "I should advise her to get married," she said. When I refused and told her positively that I could not do that, she undoubtedly went elsewhere and consulted someone more competent than myself to give advice on a matter of that kind.

Thus our good Saviour left me for some time to endure my weakness and the extreme repugnance I continued to feel for my new position, but one day, He had the goodness to come to console me in the depth of my soul. He made me understand that I should not take it so hard because I held an office that placed me in close contact with my neighbor, urging me to endeavor to receive the people who called with the same spirit of charity which animated Him when He received all who approached Him in His journeys through the cities of Judea. He also assured me that this distracting office would not hurt my soul, but on the contrary that the many labors connected with it would promote His glory.

This communication restored peace to my soul and all my previous repugnance for the position I held vanished. How merciful is God to abase Himself thus towards a poor and miserable creature, encouraging her to walk in His ways and consoling her in her troubles! Whenever this divine voice comes to instruct or to console me, it is then that I like to repeat: "Your word, Oh, Lord, is sweeter to my ear than the most beautiful music!"

Shortly thereafter our Lord fulfilled the promise He made me when He said that my distracting duties would not harm my spiritual progress but rather promote it. Briefly, I wish to speak here about several new communications which our Lord now gave me regarding the Work of Reparation, about which I have already written at great length elsewhere. In passing, I wish merely to mention here that our Lord now embued me with such intense longing to see the Work of Reparation established that I was overwhelmed with anguish so extreme that I felt unable even to partake of food. I knew I could not bear this heavy burden much longer without succumbing under its weight. For that reason I felt strongly urged to lay this whole matter at the feet of the Archbishop himself.

Our worthy superiors had in the past acquainted His Excellency with my revelations regarding the Work of Reparation, and now I too had the honor of writing to him on this subject. The Archbishop already had some small leaflets about the Association of Reparation in Rome printed recommending this Work to the priests of his diocese, but he had not as yet erected the Association.

Therefore, our Lord now made known to me that the Association which He desired to see established should have two ends in view; first, the Reparation for blasphemy, and second, the Reparation for the profanation of Sundays, since these two enormous crimes were provoking the anger of God. Seeing clearly that thus far the designs of our Lord in this Work had not been carried out, I felt urged to place this matter, which was crushing me, before the Archbishop.

Notwithstanding the natural aversion I had to make this step, I begged my superiors to ask the Archbishop to come and to honor me with his presence, despite my unworthiness, since I felt I could no longer live without speaking to him. Our worthy prelate in his charity did not delay in acceding to my request. Having had the goodness to come, he consoled me and gave me some wise counsels, assuring me that I was not laboring under any illusion concerning the revelations which I had received. He told me also that he recognized in my communications the seal of God, and that the lights with which I had been favored bore no stamp of deception.

This verdict of the Archbishop was like balm poured upon my soul, bringing me great relief. For until now, my confessor would not pronounce anything definite on the revelations I received regarding the Work of Reparation. He remained ever reticent, telling me that it belonged to the first superior in the diocese, namely, the Archbishop, who would be enlightened from the Holy Ghost, to pronounce a true judgment, and that therefore I must wait until I hear his decision.

And now at last I was convinced as never before that my

revelations came from God. And although the Archbishop gave me very little hope that he could proceed with the erection of this Association on account of the many difficulties which he told me he foresaw in this project, this did not prevent me from trusting firmly that the Work would eventually be established. Being told of the obstacles that impeded the Work, I believed that our Lord would in His own time remove all barriers so that His divine decree would be fulfilled.

The following are the reasons that helped me arrive at this conclusion. I argued thus: Since the Archbishop who had received from God the grace to pronounce judgment has assured me that the revelations given me by God in spite of my unworthiness, regarding the Work of Reparation, are not imaginary, then most assuredly this Work shall be established because the word of God is creative and unfailing, and it is this word of God which I hear in my soul and which asks this Work of me.

If, on the contrary, God would have allowed the Archbishop to tell me that all my communications were illusions, then I would have abandoned all, for by the grace of God I always had more confidence in the words of my superiors than in any interior words which I thought I heard spoken by our Lord, since in these we may sometimes be mistaken, whereas faith never makes us err. And the Saviour in speaking of superiors said: "Who hears you, hears me." We cannot, therefore, be mistaken in hearing them. These words of the holy Gospel have always impressed me and I have engraved them in my heart. Putting these words into practice, I received great graces coming to me through the medium of those who had charge of guiding my soul.

A short time after I had the honor of my interview with the Archbishop, he was pleased to approve the Prayers of Reparation, of which I have spoken, and after making a few necessary corrections, he granted his permission to have them printed. But this printing was not done immediately. In the meantime our Lord made me understand that a mere printing of the prayers alone would never suffice, but that it was necessary to add an explanation throwing light on the end which the Work had in view. The Saviour told me that in order to stimulate the interest of the Faithful to say these prayers to the glory of the Holy Name of God, it was essential to instruct them concerning the designs of God in this great Work, for only then when this would be done through the means of adequate printed matter would we see pious souls feasting themselves on these prayers as bees feast upon flowers. He then revealed to me that these prayers would be very instrumental in obtaining the conversion of sinners.

Consequently, a small booklet, containing Prayers of Reparation, and some reflections on blasphemy and the profanation of holy days, was compiled. The Archbishop approved this little work which at once met with unusual success, so that in a short time more than 25,000 of these pamphlets were distributed. From several cities came petitions to Tours asking for these prayers to the Holy Name of God, which were being recited with great fervor. Our Lord now came to me saying that this new harmony had appeased His anger, but that He still wanted the establishment of the Association exactly as He had asked for it.

At this time, a certain priest, who heard of the Work and became very much interested in it, came to visit me. He asked me to pray for two special favors, one for himself and one for a brother priest, both favors being spiritual ones, to save the souls and reputation of two young persons in whom these priests were interested. This clergyman said to me: "I already believe in the Work with which our Lord has charged you but in order to be more certain of it, I will ask you to pray for these two favors, as signs, and I promise you that if our Lord grants them, both my friend and I will devote ourselves to spread the Reparation.

Thinking that glory would accrue to our Lord if I accepted the clergyman's proposal, I promised him that I would pray for his two intentions in the spirit of obedience because whenever I asked any favor of our Lord in this manner, I obtained it more readily.

After the visiting priest left, I at once went before the Blessed Sacrament, to beg our Saviour to defend His cause in the Work of Reparation by granting the favors so much desired, since these two priests promised to become defenders of God's Holy Name blasphemed by sinners if they received the graces requested. In short, I exhausted whatever meager eloquence I had to touch the Divine Heart of the good Saviour and also began a novena for these two intentions.

Our Lord immediately attested with proof to the divine character of His Work of Reparation, for that same evening the priest who had visited our convent obtained the favor he desired while his friend obtained his a short time later. This clergyman then told us joyfully that our Lord answered his prayers beyond all expectations, for it turned out that the unfortunate happening soon redounded to the greater glory of God, and also to the happiness of all those persons so recently distressed.

Similarly in many other ways did our Lord prove that He Himself was the author of this Work of Reparation and that it was not a phantom of my imagination. Besides, it should be clear to anyone who reads this history that of myself I would never have the intelligence to invent a Work so lofty, destined to glorify God's Name and to save souls, for I am but a poor little donkey of the Holy Child Jesus. So it must follow that it was really the Holy Ghost who revealed this to me, in spite of my unworthiness. As for myself, I have a strong conviction in the depth of my soul that this Work shall one day be established.

As for the obstacles that have been raised, our Lord Himself told me that the more glorious something is in the sight of God, so much the more does the rage of the devil oppose it. The Saviour made me know that the evil spirit would do everything in his power to impede and to crush this Work. For that reason I am not at all surprised at the various difficulties encountered, for our Lord told me one day that He would allow the demon to cross His Work in order to test the fidelity of His servants. He then assured me that in spite of all the efforts of satan to annihilate the Work of Reparation, the will of our Lord to glorify the Name of His Father would be fulfilled, and His Work would be triumphantly established.

But what always astonishes me is that our Lord should have entrusted this great Work to a poor Bretonne like myself, who has but little sense, no talent, and who lacks virtue. Surely, in leaving the world, I had but one ambition and that was to become a house-servant of the Holy Family, and when later I was admitted into the convent I longed only to become the little donkey of the Divine Jesus. I was far, indeed, from imagining that when this Holy Child asked me for the ground of my soul, that He intended to build upon it such an edifice to the glory of God's Name. However, one day He made it known to me that it was precisely because of my extreme littleness that He chose me to be His instrument in order that from this He should derive greater glory.

It now also became quite clear to me why our Lord should have allowed my superiors to order me to write the story of my whole life. For surely were I to leave in writing only an account of all the exalted revelations which I received from our Lord regarding the Work of Reparation, those who would read them might be led to believe that the person to whom these communications were made must have been a very virtuous and spiritual soul who was entirely lost in the contemplation of the Divinity.

But the Holy Child Jesus desired to preserve anyone from getting such a false idea about this little servant. He wished rather that all should know her to be poor and imperfect as she really is, and for that reason He willed it that my superiors should order me to write the whole story of my life.

At first I excused myself, telling Reverend Mother that I could hardly be expected to remember the things that happened before I entered religion, and my intention was to render only a small résumé of the graces which I received from God's generosity. But knowing that obedience makes everything easy, I addressed myself to my little King, the Divine Child Jesus, in whose small hand I placed my pen, and I begged Him to write the life-story of His little donkey, in order that it might redound to the glory of His Father, and to my own confusion.

The Divine Child answered my prayer beyond all my expectations, for not only did He remind me of things which Reverend Mother wanted to know that appertained to my life before entering religion, but He, as it were, Himself wrote the whole life of this His little servant, for indeed, making known to me His will, the writing was done practically without a stop.

One day, however, I became somewhat worried, remembering that the Gospel teaches us that the right hand must not know what the left hand does. Reflecting that the record of what little virtue I practiced during life would be published about me some day, I feared losing the merit thereof. But during prayer I was given to understand that I had no cause to worry over this matter, as our Lord showed me that if I had practiced in life very great virtues, it would not have been necessary for me now to be obliged to write an account of them, for the perfume of great virtues would spread sufficiently of itself. But since, on the contrary, I had practiced only very small virtues, it was now necessary for me to write an account of them, as it were, to show them off for the greater glory of His Name.

The following comparison then suggested itself to my mind. Look at a poor man as he is assigned by a great person to undertake a mission. This poor man at once draws out from his clothes closet his very best suit, in order to make a favorable impression, sparing no pains to attire himself in the best possible fashion, in order that he might be well received by the great personage. Now, if he were really rich, it would not be in the least necessary for him to go to so much trouble, because the prestige of his titles and his wealth would suffice to insure him a favorable reception.

Thus did our Lord show me by comparison that inasmuch as I was poor, He wanted me to bring out of the clothes closet of my heart the meager stock of virtues which I had practiced with His grace in order to make myself presentable as an emissary who was obliged to negotiate a mission with which He had charged me to the glory of His Name. "These considerations," our Lord finally said to me, "will humble you and they will also serve to calm you when you are disturbed as to what you have written for the accomplishment of My designs." Given this assurance, my soul was filled with great peace.

In conclusion, I want to explain that it is to the Holy Family and also to the generosity of the Holy Child Jesus that I am indebted for the graces I received in my life despite my unworthiness. I have dedicated myself to the Divine Child to honor particularly the mysteries of His Sacred Childhood, so little appreciated in the world, and so unheeded because of the spirit of independence which is everywhere so predominant. Very often I used to beg this Divine Child to establish in my soul the Kingdom of His Holy Childhood, and to remain enthroned there according to His good pleasure and the extent of His designs in my regard. Undoubtedly, He heard my prayer, for one day while completely engrossed in thoughts about the Divine Infant, He led me also to consider the mysteries of His adult life, and finally brought me to the contemplation of His Divinity, that is, in the Work of Reparation, there to glorify the Holy Name of the Deity Himself. But the latter developments in my meditations do not prevent me from feeling that my soul is ever dedicated and bound to honor particularly the Mysteries of the Divine Childhood.

Yes, the Holy Child is my model, my strength, my consolation; in short, He is the complete joy of my heart. He is my model of patience and resignation, Who teaches me by His example, as He rests silently in the crib, content to wait thirty-three years before consuming His sacrifice, to the glory of His Father, for the salvation of the world. Thus He teaches me that in the Work of Reparation I must also be resigned to wait in patience for its triumph until the moment decreed by God at last arrives. Therefore I am content to wait together with Him, and I suffer together with Him.

But what was the chief occupation of Jesus during His Childhood, I ask myself. The answer is that He was ever intent on glorifying God's Holy Name. "Did you not know," He said to His Mother, when she found Him in the temple, "that I must be about My Father's business?" Therefore, I repeatedly ask this Divine Child to teach me how I must glorify the Name of His Father. I beg Him to recite together with me that prayer which He Himself offered to His Father while He lived on earth: "My Father glorify Your Name," and then I add, "in the Work of Reparation." At other times I present myself before Him, saying: "Lord Jesus, You are a most merciful judge, and I come to You Who have received from Your Father the power to exercise all judgment. Although I am not worthy that You plead my cause, yet I ask You, for the glory of the Holy Name of God, to defend my case. Say only one word and my case shall be won in this Work destined to give glory to the Divine Majesty. Speak, sweet Jesus, to Your Father. And You, Oh, Eternal Father, glorify Your name, and rebuke the demon who dares to blaspheme this, Your Most Holy Name. Satan, begone!"

Whenever I prayed in that manner I felt that the devil was highly incensed against me for he dislikes being brought to judgment, and out of revenge he plunged my soul, one day, into a fearful state. But I prayed to our Lord as follows: "Give me Your sustaining grace, Jesus my spouse, for hoping in You alone, I will continue to despise the infernal spirit and all his wicked blasphemies by which he thinks he can frighten me. Never will I cease to call on You as the Just Judge, but rather I will the more steadfastly persevere in this prayer: "Lord, You have been appointed by the Eternal Father to exercise all judgment, and I now beg You to overthrow my adversary by a verdict of Your judgment, remembering that You have promised that God would avenge His elect who call on Him night and day, and that He will surely come to their assistance."

Sit Nomen Domini benedictum!
Vade retro, Satana!

SISTER MARY OF ST. PETER
AND OF THE HOLY FAMILY,
UNWORTHY CARMELITE

JUNE 13, 1847

[106]

PART II

REVELATIONS
ON THE WORK OF REPARATION
GIVEN BY OUR LORD
TO
SISTER MARY OF ST. PETER
AND OF THE HOLY FAMILY

REVELATION OF APRIL, 1843

In this Revelation our Lord emphasizes the necessity of honoring both the Heart of Jesus and the Heart of Mary. He urges souls never to separate these two hearts.

DURING MY LAST RETREAT it was judged opportune by my superiors to command me to write a brief summary of the supernatural favors which I had received from God in spite of my extreme unworthiness. Thus the prioress said to me:

"Sister, since God has withdrawn from you His extraordinary favors, perhaps it is because you have proved yourself unfaithful to Him. Offer to Him, therefore, acts of repentance for your infidelities and beg Him to restore your soul to that state which you enjoyed in the past, when He so often revealed Himself to you."

I obeyed and begged our Lord to forgive me my faults. At that particular time, however, my soul was extremely perturbed and it was difficult for me to pray at all. My imagination was like a runaway horse that I could not control. Nevertheless I implored the Saviour to restore my soul to a state of prayerful meditation since the prioress had ordered me to ask for this grace.

Our Lord at once had the goodness to hear my prayer addressed to Him through obedience for I believe it was on the following morning, as I awoke, that I heard an interior voice saying:

"Return to the house of your Father which is none other than My Heart."

These words produced a great peace in my soul. As soon as I entered the choir for mental prayer, I united myself to our Lord in the Blessed Sacrament, and immediately I heard Him say to me:

"Apply yourself diligently to honor My Sacred Heart and also the Heart of My Mother. Never separate these two hearts. It is My desire that you pray to these two hearts for yourself and for sinners. I in turn will forget your past faults and furthermore I will grant you even more graces than before because you are now more completely united to Me through your Vows."

As there arose within me a doubt as to whether it was really our Lord Who had spoken to me, I then heard Him say:

"It is I, Jesus, present in the Blessed Sacrament Who speaks to you. I have various ways of communicating with souls. Are you not able to perceive how calm and how united your soul is to Me at present, whereas only recently it was a prey to many distractions? Begin to do as I tell you and you will soon experience many beneficial results."

After that our Lord made me understand that I should not become attached to a devotion which gratifies the senses merely, and He gave me the light to see that people often follow after interior sweetness, thinking that they are following after Him.

Fulfilling our Lord's command, I began fervently to honor those two loving Hearts of Jesus and Mary interiorly, and also exteriorly by embroidering pictures of these two hearts on scapulars, begging our Lord to save those who would wear them.

I also said to our Saviour at this time, "I do not seek consolations in prayer, Oh, Lord. All I care for is Your glory and the salvation of souls." Then offering my will to the Father, my memory to the Son, and my understanding to the Holy

Ghost, I delivered myself entirely into the hands of God, and I understood that He intended to purify my soul through interior suffering.

Thus I was plunged into a gloom, and groping in darkness I was assailed by many temptations. But my worst suffering arose from my unbounded longing to love and glorify God. Nothing that I could do was able to satisfy me, and so I continued hungering for God, feeling within me my utter insufficiency, my sinfulness and my misery. Only God sustained me during this trial and yet I felt that I would not have exchanged this suffering for even the sweetest consolations, desiring only the glory of God and the salvation of souls.

In the meantime, not the least of my sufferings were those caused by the demon of blasphemy. Clinging to the cross while the tempest raged, I finally made bold to speak to God these words, "Oh, my God, You must know by now that I realize fully my nothingness and my misery!" By these words I meant to say, "It is enough, my God! As long as I shall live I will know how to acknowledge Your gifts. Never shall I attribute them to myself because I am absolutely convinced that I myself am only indigence and nothingness!"

Interiorly urged to turn to our holy mother St. Teresa for help, I began a novena in her honor, and before it was finished, something happened to me which I will now relate.

REVELATION OF AUGUST 26, 1843

Sister Mary of St. Peter receives the first Revelation concerning the sins of blasphemy. To atone for this outrageous crime, the Saviour inspires the nun to recite often a prayer of praise to the Holy Name of God, which He dictated, entitled "THE GOLDEN ARROW."

ON AUGUST 26, 1843 (the day after the Feast of St. Louis, the crusader against blasphemy), there was a terrible storm during which I felt the justice of an angry God as I had never before felt it in my life. Kneeling, so that my forehead touched the ground, I ceaselessly offered our Saviour, Jesus Christ, to His Eternal Father, for the expiation of my sins and for the needs of Holy Church.

Since one of the nuns in our convent experienced on that day the same emotion as I did, when the hour for evening prayer arrived, I placed myself in spirit at the foot of the cross, and approaching our Lord familiarly, I spoke to Him about the incident of the storm. After that I asked Him to tell me the reason why I felt so strongly on that day the roused anger of His Eternal Father.

Although recently I had experienced much aridity in prayer, now as soon as I had addressed our Saviour, He at once relaxed His manner towards me and said:

"My daughter, I have heard your sighs and your groans, and I have also witnessed your ardent desire to glorify Me, which desire does not spring from yourself, for it is I Who have given it birth in your soul."

Then gathering the powers of my soul, our Lord opened His Heart to me and said:

[112]

"My Name is everywhere blasphemed! There are even children who blaspheme!"

He then made me see that this frightful sin wounds His divine Heart more grievously than all other sins, showing me how by blasphemy the sinner curses Him to His Face, attacks Him publicly, nullifies his redemption, and pronounces his own judgment and condemnation.

Our Lord then made me visualize the act of blasphemy as a poisoned arrow continually wounding His divine Heart. After that He revealed to me that He wanted to give me a "Golden Arrow" which would have the power of wounding Him delightfully, and which would also heal those other wounds inflicted by the malice of sinners.

The following is the formula of the "Golden Arrow" which is an Act of Praise that our Lord Himself dictated to me, notwithstanding my unworthiness, for the reparation of blasphemy against His Holy Name:

THE GOLDEN ARROW

May the most holy, most sacred, most adorable, most incomprehensible and unutterable Name of God be always praised, blessed, loved, adored and glorified in heaven, on earth and in the hells, by all the creatures of God and by the Sacred Heart of our Lord Jesus Christ in the Most Holy Sacrament of the Altar. AMEN.

Since I felt somewhat astonished at the words which our Lord used when He said to me, "in the hells," He made me understand that His Justice was also glorified there. I furthermore beg that notice be taken of this that our Lord did not say to me "in hell" (*dans l'enfer*), but He said, "in the hells" (*dans les enfers*), which can be understood to include also purgatory where He is loved and glorified by His suffering souls. Then too, the word "hell" applies not only to the abode of the reprobate, for faith teaches us that our Lord Himself after His death decended into hell, which was the place where the souls of the just awaited Him. Besides, does not Holy Church pray her Divine Spouse to deliver the souls of her children from the gates of hell? *A porta inferi, erue Domine, animas eorum* (Office of the Dead).*

After our Lord finished dictating this prayer which He called the "Golden Arrow" He added a warning:

"Be careful to utilize this grace because I shall demand an account of it from you," and at that moment I believe I saw streaming from the Sacred Heart of Jesus, delightfully wounded by this "Golden Arrow," torrents of graces for the conversion of sinners. This vision encouraged me to address our Saviour as follows, "My Lord, are you then giving me charge of blasphemers?" But it was not then the will of the Saviour to disclose anything further to me on this subject.

After that, reflecting that God must indeed be angered because of the blasphemies of which men were guilty, yet at the same time feeling my weakness, and fearing also the demon, I begged the Blessed Virgin to take charge of the mission which her divine Son entrusted to me.

Ever since this revelation on the "Golden Arrow" I have felt my soul completely changed, and wholly occupied in glorifying the Most Holy Name of God. In addition to the "Golden Arrow" our Lord also inspired me to compose a little exercise of Reparation in the form of twenty-four Acts of Adoration to atone for the blasphemies uttered each hour of the day. Our Lord later had the goodness to reveal to me that this exercise of Reparation which I performed was agreeable to Him, and

---

* *In nomine Jesu omne genu flectatur, caelestium, terrestrium, et infernorum* — In the name of Jesus let every knee bow of those that are in heaven, on earth, and under the earth. St. Paul, PHIL. : 2, 10.

that He desired this devotion to be spread everywhere. The Saviour then made me share His own ardent longing to see the Name of His Eternal Father glorified. He further made me understand that just as the Angels sing, Sanctus, Sanctus, Sanctus, without ceasing, so must I apply myself to glorifying His Holy Name. By doing this, He assured me that I would fulfill the command which He had given me a short while ago when He told me to honor His Sacred Heart and also the heart of His holy Mother, for these two hearts were continually being wounded by blasphemy.

In addition, He also made me comprehend that this devotion would not hinder me from honoring Him in His Mysteries as I was accustomed to do, because in all the Mysteries of His life, His Heart has ever suffered from this crime of blasphemy.

I again forcibly understood, however, that the more agreeable anything is to God, the more bitter does the demon try to make it so that the soul may become discouraged, but that such obstacles only increase our merit if we are faithful and if we persevere to the end. Our Lord gave me all these instructions in order to sustain me in the trials which I would suffer from Satan on account of this Work of Reparation. In fact, our Saviour told me that Satan would do all in his power to crush and annihilate this Work but that all his efforts would prove in vain.

REVELATION OF SEPTEMBER 29, 1843

Our Lord announces that He desires the Work of Reparation to be spread by means of the press. He assures Sister Mary that this Devotion contains nothing that is not in conformity with the spirit of the Church.

DURING EVENING PRAYER on the Feast of St. Michael, September 29, our Lord gathering the powers of my soul made me understand that the twenty-four short exercises of Reparation which I have composed and which I recite were pleasing to His Divine Heart, and that these prayers made Him forget all my faults.

As our Reverend Mother was at that time very ill, I prayed for her recovery, but our Lord made known to me that if the community desired to obtain such improvement in Reverend Mother's health as would enable her to perform the duties incumbent on her office, we must make a Novena of Reparation for blasphemies uttered against God's Holy Name, before the Blessed Sacrament, by reciting in addition to the "Golden Arrow" the Twenty-four Exercises which He had inspired me to compose a short time ago. Our Lord also made known to me that it was only proper for children to help their mother, and that if we rendered this satisfaction to His Heart, He would open It and pour out a torrent of graces on our community.

I felt I could not possibly refuse to carry out this order of our Saviour, especially when, as an inducement, He now added: "Oh, if you only knew what I have done for you and how much I have cared for your soul, you would be truly astonished to see the Creator abasing Himself so profoundly towards a mere creature!"

I, therefore, replied, "Oh, Lord, although I will risk receiving humiliations, nevertheless, I pledge myself to deliver Your message, knowing that You will be glorified by this Novena."

Placing myself under Mary's protection, I reported this communication of our Lord to the prioress, who on that day was suffering most acutely. Because of the violent pains she at once gave her consent for the community to make this Novena. On my part, I never had cause to regret any effort I made in this Work which aimed at honoring the Name of our Lord, for He never allows Himself to be outdone in generosity.

On that same day, which was the Feast of St. Michael, the Saviour made known to me that He desired our Reverend Mother to get busy with the matter of circulating the Prayers of Reparation, for He wanted this Devotion to be spread. As a guarantee of the genuineness of my mission, He promised me an improvement in the prioress' health. I then felt encouraged to promise Him in return that if He, indeed, cured our Mother that she, on her part, would not neglect His Work of Reparation. At the end of the Novena, the prioress received the favor which our Lord had promised, and since her health was now so much better, I said to our Saviour, "Dear Lord, I will never hesitate to perform whatever errands You may have for me to do."

At that time our Lord also assured me that this Devotion of Reparation contained nothing contrary to the spirit of the Church, saying that, indeed, what else is the Church ever doing if not continually glorifying the Holy Name of God?

Ever since that time, He has even more deeply plunged me into the work of making reparation for blasphemy. Moreover, since He continued to press me to ask that these Prayers of Reparation be published and circulated, I relayed His messages in spite of the extreme repugnance I felt in bringing this matter to my superior's attention. Each time that I did so, I felt my soul relieved of a heavy burden.

REVELATION OF NOVEMBER 3, 1843

*Our Lord discloses to Sister Mary of St. Peter
that it is His Will that the Carmelite Community of
Tours should give birth to the new Devotion of
Reparation since they have been offering special
prayers for the intention that the designs
of the Sacred Heart be fulfilled.*

IT BEING the First Friday, November 3, I had the privilege of
receiving Holy Communion for the special intention that the
designs of the Sacred Heart of Jesus should be accomplished.
This was being done in our convent to fulfill a certain vow
which our Reverend Mother had made, promising God that
for a whole year two of the religious in her community would
offer their Communions for this intention.

As soon as the Blessed Sacrament was exposed on this First
Friday, our Lord said to me:

"Since the Community prays for the fulfillment of the designs of My Sacred Heart, it is only right that it should have
the honor of giving birth to this new devotion, the Work of
Reparation," making me understand that we are to promote
this Work by means of the press, that is by printing and
circulating the Prayers of Reparation for blasphemy.

Then something very extraordinary, and most difficult to
explain, took place within me. I felt my soul deposited in the
Heart of Jesus and as though surrounded by the fire of love. It
seemed to me for some moments that my soul had left my
miserable body, in order to become reunited to its God. Vividly
conscious that God was both the principle and the end of my

[119]

being, my soul felt itself happily lost in God. In this state I felt myself unable any longer to act, yet interiorly I continued to pray, saying, "My God, how wonderful are Your works! I see that You are not, after all, such a hidden God." I felt like adding, "Lord, it is good to remain here. Let us build three tabernacles and imprison in them the three faculties of my soul: my memory, my will and my understanding."

Such was my experience all during Holy Mass. Then having received Holy Communion, I took the liberty to address our Lord as follows: "Oh, my dear Saviour, now that through Communion I am even nearer to You, will You have the kindness to repeat all that You told me at the beginning of Holy Mass?"

But I saw that our Lord was not inclined to do what I had asked Him at that moment, and therefore, I surrendered to what He was then operating within me, which produced the happy feeling of being absorbed by God, of which I have spoken above.

After a short while, however, our Lord told me that He purposely remained silent in order to teach me by this that it was not at all in my power to hear interior words whenever I chose. He also told me that the extraordinary favor of feeling myself lost in God, which I experienced during Holy Mass, was to serve as proof that it was really He Himself Who acted in my soul, and that I should not fear the presence herein of the wicked spirit. Having given me this short lesson, our Lord then said:

"My daughter, in placing obstacles to My plans over your soul, you have offended Me more and grieved My Heart more deeply than all your Sisters put together. I am not mentioning your frailty on this point in order to worry you. Trust Me, for I will forget all your faults if you will but lovingly, and with zeal, work for the interests of My glory, overcoming all obstacles. The two reasons why I desire to make use of you are, first, because you are so puny, and second, because you have offered yourself to Me for the accomplishment of My plans. This offering has won My Heart. Be humble and simple and make known your littleness for that will only serve to advance My interests," and He made me understand that it was His desire to sanctify me.

He then spoke words of great encouragement, for whereas until now He had repeatedly commanded me to tell my superiors how much He desired them to have the Prayers of Reparation published and circulated, on this occasion He gave me the following promise:

"Daughter, be consoled, for these Prayers of Reparation shall be printed and circulated!"

REVELATION OF APPROXIMATELY
NOVEMBER 10, 1843

Our Lord makes known that it is His Will that the Community of Tours make a Novena in Reparation for the contempt and outrageous blasphemies hurled against the Holy Name of God, and He again strongly urges the Community to print and disseminate the Prayers of Reparation.

THE SAVIOUR has had the goodness to communicate Himself to me, and He told me to ask if Reverend Mother would be willing to snatch the sword from His hands, since the spouses have full power over the Bridegroom. In order to do this, He asks that the Community make a Novena of Reparation using a formula of prayers similar to the first one made to obtain her cure. But the Saviour insisted however, that this Novena be made entirely in a spirit of Reparation for the outrageous blasphemies of which our nation is guilty and for the specific intention of obtaining mercy.

Our Saviour also said that since He chose the Community of Tours to be the first to learn of His sighs and His desires for the establishment of this Work, it was only fitting that from this Community He should likewise expect to reap His first consolations through their Novena of Reparation.

He urged me once more to ask that the prayers of atonement for blasphemies be printed and disseminated, emphasizing that it was His desire, however, that this Community should defray the expenses incurred in the printing, so that later He could shower upon this Carmel His greatest blessings and repay it a hundredfold for the amount of money spent.

I, therefore, beg once more, in the Name of Jesus, that this should be done, and we will see how He shall take care of all our needs. Truly, I can carry this heavy burden no longer. I beg, therefore, that this matter be seriously examined before God, and now having made these declarations, I believe my errand is completed, and my soul feels relieved.

REVELATION OF APPROXIMATELY
NOVEMBER 15, 1843

Our Lord repays Sister Mary of St. Peter for recit-
ing the Chaplet of Reparation by granting her a
vision in which He presents her in turn with Beads
of precious stones, mounted on a chain of gold.

OUR LORD inspired me at this time to compose certain prayers
of reparation in the form of a Chaplet, or a small rosary.
This Chaplet is made up of thirty-three small beads, on which
is recited thirty-three times the prayer, "Arise, Oh, Lord, and
let Your enemies be scattered, and let those that hate You flee
before Your Face," and also six large beads on which are
recited the ejaculation, "My Jesus, mercy," followed by the
doxology, "Glory be to the Father, etc."

One day after Holy Mass our Lord appeared to me presenting me with a similar Chaplet which I saw was made of
precious stones strung on a fine gold chain. Deeming myself
quite unworthy of possessing such a treasure, I begged the
Blessed Virgin to keep this beautiful rosary for me by placing
it in her Immaculate Heart, and I also begged our Lord to
attach indulgences to the recitation of this Chaplet.

REVELATION OF APPROXIMATELY
NOVEMBER 18, 1843

*Our Lord assures Sister Mary of St. Peter that the
Holy Angels would finally secure the triumph of the
Work of Reparation in spite of the vicious attempts
made by the wicked angels to endeavor at every cost
to crush the Work at its roots.*

ONE DAY during prayer, our Lord warned me in advance about
the fury of Satan against this holy devotion, but He also consoled me, saying:

"I give you My Name to be your light in the darkness and
your strength in battle. Satan will do all in his power to crush
this Work at its roots. But I assure you that the Holy Name of
God will triumph, and it will be the Holy Angels who will
gain the victory in the conflict."

REVELATION OF NOVEMBER 20, 1843

Our Lord again urges Sister Mary of St. Peter to abandon herself as a complete victim to God for the accomplishment of His plans. Therefore He tells her once more to seek the permission of her superiors to make this Act of Self-Oblation.

ON THE EVE of the day of the renewal of my vows, November 20, having made a spiritual Communion, I became aware of the presence of the Holy Child Jesus in my soul, Who urged me once again to offer Him an act of perfect sacrifice of myself for the accomplishment of His plans. For this Act of Oblation our Lord had first asked me a few days after I had entered the convent, that is, about four years ago. At that time, one morning after receiving Holy Communion, I saw our Lord Who was accompanied by an Angel. Then I was given a vision in which I saw hell. After that our Lord spoke to me saying that He wanted me to offer myself entirely to Him, and that I should willingly promise to endure everything He might send me, in order that His special plans might be accomplished. He furthermore wanted me to surrender to Him whatever merits I might gain in my new career, for this same end, namely, that His designs might be fulfilled.

At the same time He made me comprehend that He Himself would look after my interests, that He would allow me to share His merits, and that He would Himself become the director of my soul. The Angel at His side urged me to consent to so magnificent a proposal, and he even seemed envious of my good fortune. He appeared in a way to regret not having a body, giving me to understand that whereas it was possible for me to acquire merit, he himself was unable to do so. Furthermore, this heavenly spirit told me that if I gave my consent to our Lord's proposal, the holy angels would surround my bed at my death and would defend me from the snares of the demon.

Although I felt strongly attracted to make this Act at once, I did not do so right away. I decided instead to wait until I could receive the advice of the Mistress of Novices, who was also the Prioress, but after speaking to her, she in her wisdom answered me, "My child, the Act of Sacrifice to our Lord which you ask my permission to make is not an ordinary one. Since you are only a postulant, and as yet I have no right over you, I cannot permit it."

I was to be refused more than once, and although I felt myself forcibly drawn to make this act of complete self-abandonment, yet one thing was always lacking and that was permission.

Finally it happened that on March 25 of that year, being the Feast of the Annunciation, I wrote out an Act of Self-Oblation which I made, offering myself to the Child Jesus, but He now made me understand that I had received permission to make this Act only partially, because I had not explained to my superior the true nature of this oblation, and that as a result He accepted it only as a simple and ordinary act of dedication, and nothing more. Furthermore, the Divine Child made me understand that if I really wanted my soul to be entirely His in order that He could work in it all that He desired, it was necessary for me to ask my superiors again for their full consent.

I therefore approached my superiors begging them to allow me to make this Act of Sacrifice the next day, November 21, the Feast of the Presentation, but our worthy superiors again refused me permission. Our Lord then seemed satisfied with my good will, for I saw now that this would not prevent Him from giving me His Revelations concerning the great Work of Reparation.

REVELATION OF NOVEMBER 24, 1843

THE FEAST OF ST. JOHN OF THE CROSS

It being the Feast of the great Carmelite Reformer, St. John of the Cross, the Saviour reveals to Sr. Mary that the profanation of Sundays together with blasphemies are the crimes that have reached a peak of wickedness. Pleading for the establishment of the Work of Reparation, our Lord says: "Oh, to whom shall I address myself if not to a Carmelite whose very vocation obliges her unceasingly to glorify My Name?"

IMMEDIATELY AFTER receiving Holy Communion on the Feast of our holy father, St. John of the Cross, our Lord seized possession of the powers of my soul and made me hear the following words:

"Until now I have shown you only in part the plans of My Heart but today I want to reveal them to you in all their fullness." He then continued:

"The whole earth is covered with crimes and the violation of the first three of the Ten Commandments of God has aroused the anger of My Father. The crimes that fill up the cup of wickedness are blasphemies against God's Holy Name and the profanation of Sundays. These sins have reached to the very throne of Almighty God, and they have provoked His wrath which is about to strike everywhere unless His Justice be appeased. Never before have these crimes reached such a peak." After that our Lord said:

"I desire, and this most urgently, that there be formed to

[129]

honor the Name of My Father an Association, properly approved and well organized. Your superiors have good reasons to take only such steps in this devotion which are well founded, for otherwise My designs would not be fulfilled."

Since I had never heard of any association in the Church similar to the one for which our Lord now asked, I therefore said to Him, "Oh, my God, if I only were sure that it is really You Who speaks to me, I would not hesitate to tell all these things to my superiors." To this He replied:

"It is up to them and not up to you to make certain of this. Besides, have I not often in the past communicated with your soul in the same way as I do at this moment? Take care, therefore, because if you should fail in simplicity and place obstacles to My plans, you shall be held responsible for the salvation of souls. On the other hand, if you are faithful, your crown will be enriched."

Then our Lord made me hear clearly that it was His desire to bestow mercy upon sinners by instituting this Work of Reparation. And as a parting remark He said to me:

"Oh, to whom shall I address myself if not to a Carmelite whose very vocation obliges her unceasingly to glorify My Name?"

While this was taking place, I felt my soul entirely lost in God, and simultaneously I was overcome by awe as our Lord made me realize the meaning of the words spoken to Abraham, that if there could be found at least ten just souls, God would spare the guilty cities for the sake of these ten just. It also seemed to me that for the sake of those who would practice Reparation for the sins committed against the majesty of God, His justice would be appeased and He would grant mercy to the guilty.

REVELATION OF DECEMBER 7, 1843

VIGIL OF THE FEAST OF THE IMMACULATE CONCEPTION

Our Lord confides to Sr. Mary that whereas He would still endure patiently the contempt shown Him by sinners, He was roused to anger by the present outrages committed against His Eternal Father. The Saviour then insists that since blasphemy is universal and public, Reparation for this crime must likewise be public, and it must be extended to all the cities.

MY SOUL is terrified at what our Lord has just made me hear during prayer this morning, charging me with the duty of transmitting His message to my superiors without any fear of being deceived. He said He was incensed with anger against our nation, and that He has sworn in His wrath to avenge Himself if Reparation to the honor of His Divine Father were not made for all the blasphemies of which the people are guilty, making me hear that He could no longer remain among men who, like vipers, were tearing at the entrails of His mercy. He said that as for the contempt shown to Himself, He would still endure it patiently, but that He was roused to anger by the outrages committed against His Eternal Father. He then declared that His Mercy was on the verge of giving way to His Justice, and that His wrath would overflow with a fury such as had never yet been heard of before.

Greatly frightened, I pleaded, "My Lord, permit me to ask

You if You would grant our nation pardon if this Atonement for which You ask were made to God?"

Our Lord answered me:

"Yes, I will grant it pardon once more, but mark my word, once! And since this crime of blasphemy extends over the *whole* nation, and since it is *public,* I demand that Reparation be extended to *all the cities* of the nation, and that it be *public.* Woe to those cities that will not make this Reparation!"

Now it so happened that at this time, through a mere co-incidence I learned that there already existed in Rome an Association whose aim was to atone for blasphemy and that the Holy Father had granted to it a Brief under date of August 8, 1843. This was a great consolation to me, for I now felt doubly certain that the Work with which I had been entrusted, was indeed the Work of God. Moreover, I was filled with wonder at the remarkable concurrence of dates, for it was on August 26, 1843, only about two weeks after the formation of this Roman society that to me, a poor Carmelite in France, had been revealed the great Work of Reparation.

FEAST OF THE PURIFICATION

Our Lord offers a promise of pardon in view of the efforts made to spread the Reparation. He further designates St. Michael, St. Martin and St. Louis, as the special patrons of the Work, and asks that the members wear a cross, and band themselves together as "Defenders of God's Holy Name."

DURING the past several weeks I have not experienced anything extraordinary regarding the Work of Reparation, except that our Lord continued to unite Himself to me in order to make reparation and to glorify His Eternal Father.

Today, however, being the Feast of the Purification, it was my turn to receive Communion in fulfillment of the vow made by our prioress, for the intention that the designs of the Sacred Heart of Jesus be accomplished. After receiving Communion, the good Saviour had the kindness to speak to me.

Now although in the previous revelation, our Lord told me about His anger which was aroused on account of the crimes committed against His Father, which communication had left me in a frightful state of worry, and had caused me to weep, today He filled my soul with joy by making known to me the satisfaction His Divine Heart experiences at seeing the zeal and the desires of His children for this growing Association. He told me that just as His holy Mother has adopted the Arch-Confraternity of the Heart of Mary, to obtain the conversion of sinners, so will He adopt the Arch-Confraternity of Reparation. Both must go hand in hand, the one making reparation for crimes committed against God, and the other to obtain pardon, and the former would belong especially to Jesus while the other would belong especially to Mary.

Then our Lord told me that the Confraternity of Reparation which He desired to have established was to have a two-fold purpose, the first being Reparation for blasphemy, and the second being Reparation for the profanation of Sunday, since these were the two principal sins which in modern times were provoking the anger of God.

Therefore the new Association was to differ from that in Rome in that besides striving for the extirpation of blasphemy, the Rules would oblige members to refrain from all Sunday work themselves, and to do what lay in their power to see that others stop all unnecessary servile works on the holy days of the Lord.

Our Saviour also desires that this Association be placed under the patronage of St. Michael, St. Martin, and of St. Louis, asking that each member should say daily one Our Father, one Hail Mary, and one Glory be, together with the Act of Praise, called the Golden Arrow, which the Saviour had previously dictated to me. But on Sunday and on feast days, all the Prayers of Reparation are to be recited, in order to make fitting reparation for the crimes committed against God's Majesty on these days of the Lord in order to obtain mercy for the guilty.

Our Lord showed me this Association as an army of brave soldiers, uniting themselves to Him as to their Commander-in-Chief, to defend the glory of His Father. It is His Will that this militia be called "The Defenders of the Holy Name of God," so that this noble title should give evidence of the high calling of those enrolled.

Finally, our Lord told me that He desired each member of the Association to wear a special cross, and that on one side of this cross should be engraved the words, "Blessed be the Name of God," and on the reverse side should be the words, "Begone, Satan!" To all those wearing this holy cross our Lord promised a special resourcefulness to conquer the demon of blasphemy, adding that every time one hears a curse, he should repeat the two short inscriptions written on each side of the cross, and he will thus overcome the evil one and render glory to God.

At the end our Lord warned me, saying that the demon would do everything in his power to crush this Work which springs from the Sacred Heart. I then felt that I would willingly shed the last drop of my blood for such a holy association.

Our Lord also made me understand that He had not spoken to me regarding this Work for a long time because there was no need for Him to do so, and since He never does anything superfluous, He had kept silence. On this day, however, He felt it necessary to speak to me in order to show me the difference between the Confraternity of Reparation stemming from Italy, and the new Confraternity which He now demanded be formed in France, whose additional feature embodied reparation for the profanation of Sunday.

REVELATION OF FEBRUARY 25, 1844

Our Lord repeats His desire that a Confraternity of Reparation be formed so that He could avail Himself of the merits of this Association and grant pardon to the guilty who were provoking God's anger.

OUR LORD made known to me that only Reparation could disarm the Justice of God because the guilt of men had provoked His anger.

"I, therefore, demand, and most urgently, that this Work be established," our Lord said, making me understand that His Sacred Heart desires through this means to bestow mercy on mankind.

I also seem to hear this Divine Jesus from the depths of the Tabernacle addressing us with these words:

"Oh, you, who are my friends, and my faithful children, look and see if there be any sorrow like mine. Everywhere My enemies despise and insult both my Eternal Father and My Church, the cherished Spouse of My Heart. Will no one rise up to console Me by defending the glory of My Father, and the honor of My Spouse, which has been so cruelly attacked? I can no longer remain in the midst of a people that will continue to be so heedless and so ungrateful. Look at the torrents of tears that stream from My eyes! Can I find no one to wipe away these tears by making reparation to My Father, and imploring forgiveness for the guilty?"

Here is yet another comparison which God placed in my soul. Should a king, or only an ambassador, be treated with contempt by a foreign power, the whole nation at once rushes to avenge the insult, as troops are called to take up arms, and if in the conflict even many soldiers are killed, their loss is regarded as a small matter when compared to the wrong avenged.

Now let us consider how the impious insult the Holy Name of God, the King of Kings, as also how countless sinners profane the Sabbath. Yet no one bothers or troubles himself about it. For that reason our Lord Himself, the Divine Ambassador to the Kingdom of Heaven, comes down to urge us to make reparation to the honor of His Father, threatening to declare war, by sending us grave punishments if we neglect to do this. Shall we still waver in our choice? I therefore very humbly beg that the Reverend Mother ask the Archbishop to kindly attend to this. Make known to him also all the extraordinary occurrences that transpired in my soul since the feast of St. Louis on the subject of Reparation. Also kindly confer with the convent's superior to determine whether it would not be contrary to humility if I myself were to write to His Excellency, for I urgently desire to do this, and humbly solicit the permission. I feel that by writing personally to him, I shall have done everything in my power for the accomplishment of this Work. However, I would write to His Excellency only when I feel my soul under the influence of the Holy Ghost, for I would not attempt it through only my ordinary natural resourcefulness, since I consider that of myself I am capable of doing nothing.

REMARK — Having been accorded the honor of corresponding with the Archbishop, this prelate had some leaflets printed, bearing his approbation under date of March 15, 1844. These leaflets were similar to those used by the Association stemming from Italy. Recommending that Association to the pastors and other religious of his diocese, the Archbishop declared that he hoped "it would stimulate the interest of the faithful and thus help to end the outrages against the Divine Majesty." A large number of these leaflets on Reparation have been circulated, but as to the Confraternity for which our Lord has been asking, no steps have been taken for its erection. It seems that the hour has not yet arrived. Let us in silence adore the designs of God.

REVELATION OF FEBRUARY 27, 1844

Our Lord reveals to Sister Mary a method by which she is to become the spiritual ambassador of her country to intercede before God and to beg Him to show mercy to the guilty.

THE FOLLOWING is what transpired in my soul today after Holy Communion. Our Lord told me to receive Him in the Sacred Host as King, and to offer Him my soul for His dominion. He then urged me to present myself before Him in the name of our nation, as an ambassador offering Him my Communion in the spirit of reparation for the crimes of which our nation is guilty, particularly those against the Divine Majesty, and those against holy Church.

Having received this Divine King, I earnestly laid before Him the spiritual needs of our country. Then He, communicating Himself further to me, told me that He entrusted the country of France to my care, appointing me as its ambassador, so that I could negotiate about terms of peace with Him. He said that to acquit myself of this important post, I must in great humility remain at His feet in the Most Blessed Sacrament, praying for our country and for the establishment of the Work of Reparation.

He next instructed me to examine seriously the weighty role an ambassador must fulfill, warning me to remember that when such an ambassador leaves a country, it is the signal for war, and that therefore I must not voluntarily retire from His presence in the Blessed Sacrament, but at least in spirit remain there in the name of France.

I, therefore, answered Him by saying, "My God, I have given myself entirely to You for the accomplishment of Your designs. Do in me as You will." Accepting the obligations which God had now imposed on me I begged Him to make me worthy of His designs or, better still, to accomplish Himself His Will within me.

As for this adoration of Jesus in the Blessed Sacrament, for several days now, our Lord keeps me so united to Him in the Eucharist, that even on leaving the choir to attend to my various duties, I am in spirit uninterruptedly at the foot of the altar where I leave my heart. Thus, no matter in which part of the house I find myself, I am always in sight of Him, keeping Him company. Such is the interior exercise which our Lord asks of me, for it is His Will that I remain ever before the Blessed Sacrament, in the name of our country, praying for it continuously.

REVELATION OF MARCH 16, 1844

Our Lord describes to Sister Mary the enormity of the sins of blasphemy, and again demands that the Work of Reparation be established, saying that this Work surpasses various other devotions.

The Saviour also asks Sister Mary of St. Peter the pointed question: "Do you want to walk in My ways?" When she replies, "Yes," He rewards her by saying: "Consider this one of the most beautiful days of your life."

DURING holy Mass our Lord showed me the enormity of the crime of blasphemy, saying to me:

"You cannot comprehend the malice and abomination of this sin. If My Justice were not restrained by My Mercy, indeed, it would instantly crush the guilty. In fact, all creatures, even those that are inanimate, would avenge this outrage against their Creator's majesty, but I have an eternity in which to punish the guilty."

After saying this, our Lord made me understand the excellence of the Work of Reparation and He made me see how the Devotion of Reparation surpasses other devotions, how pleasing it is to God, as also to the Angels and Saints, and how beneficial it is to the Church.

Our Lord however warned me that I should not be disappointed if I did not feel any particular gratifying emotions while reciting the Prayers of Reparation. He also told me that the demon would give me an aversion for this devotion, but that these things should not worry me.

"Oh, if you only knew what great merit you acquire by saying even once, 'Admirable is the Name of God,' in the spirit of reparation for blasphemy!"

The second communication which I received from our Lord was during night prayers. I felt quite unhappy while recalling all my imperfections and therefore approaching our Lord with confidence, I uncovered to Him my great needs. He told me in answer that when a good person who is also very rich makes the acquaintance of a poor one, there is occasion for rejoicing, since the goodness and charity of such a benefactor when combined are sufficient to relieve all the other person's want and misery.

He then made me see how really needy and weak I was, and how poorly I had profited by all the graces He had sent me. Nevertheless, He was willing in His Mercy to forgive me everything. I therefore asked His pardon for my sins, and He granted it to me, saying:

"A workman cleans the tool which He wants to use."

After that our Saviour made me see to what degree a Carmelite must be divested of self and detached from everything, while she seeks only the glory of God and His Church, and the salvation of souls, which should in turn embue her with a desire for suffering and humiliations.

This Divine Saviour then taught me how of myself I could never expect to acquire these virtues, but that He Who had forgiven me all my past sins, could readily give birth to these virtues in my soul, provided I would beg Him to do this.

"Are you willing to walk in My ways?" He asked me pointedly. To this I replied, "Yes, Lord."

He then continued:

"Cast yourself blindly into My Sacred Heart. For your badge I give you the cross and the thorns that lay buried within My Heart. Do not turn away from this cross nor from these thorns because, My daughter, you are being called to a high perfection. Think therefore only of Me and in return I will think of you. Attend to My affairs and I promise you that I will take care of yours. And now, as long as you live I want you to look upon this day as one of the most beautiful days of your entire life!"

REVELATION OF MAY, 1844

Our Lord again orders Sister Mary of St. Peter to
pray for her country as its ambassador, in order to
cancel the debt incurred by guilty citizens. To pay
off this huge indebtedness He gives Himself
to her as a "Mine of Gold."

TODAY our Lord repeated the command He gave me sometime ago to pray for our nation whose shepherd He Himself is, but He said that I was chosen by Him to be a tiny shepherdess, that He gave me the mysteries of His most holy Life as my inheritance, and that from His Sacred Wounds I must draw vast treasures for my sheepfold.

In other words He said that He gave Himself to me as a "Gold Mine" with which I was to pay the debts our nation owes to the Justice of God, and He allowed me to use the great treasures concealed in His Heart. Our Lord also warned me to be very careful lest I should resemble the lazy servant of the Gospel, who buried his talents, and He added that He would demand a strict account from me.

He then went on to explain how easy it was for me to draw vast reserves of gold from this mine which, He said, He Himself had dug out of the ground by His labors and His sufferings.

I understand our Lord is ardently searching for some soul, who would but constrain Him through her prayers to have mercy on our guilty nation.

REVELATION OF JUNE 6, 1844

*Our Lord tells Sister Mary to have courage and
confidence and to engrave these two words
in her heart.*

THE WORK OF REPARATION is like a devouring fire within me
which consumes me and makes me suffer, sometimes more
and sometimes less, as it pleases God. In all my prayers I beg
our Lord to save our nation by establishing in all her cities
His Work of Reparation, and to raise up apostolic men for
this purpose. Oh, Jesus, I can do nothing for this Work since I
am but a poor and worthless creature, but accept my sufferings,
and enlighten the one who can be of service to You in this
great Work.

On the day on which it was my turn again to receive Communion in fulfillment of the vow made to the Sacred Heart, our
Lord, taking pity on my sufferings, gave me a taste of consolation, lifting my soul up for nearly two hours. In this sweet
calm He said to me:

"My child, have courage and confidence! Moreover, engrave
these two words, courage and confidence, in your heart. Oh, if
you only knew the profit which accrues to your soul from
suffering these pains, you would thank me for having given
them to you. I come to pay you a visit merely, but not to
remain with you in a way which would gratify your senses.
You shall, instead, drink the chalice, but be consoled, for
although you will not see Me, I will not be far from you. In
fact, it will be I, Myself, who will hold the chalice to your
lips while you drink it, and after this trial is past, I will again

allow you to taste My consolations. You have deserved these sufferings through your many infidelities; however, it is not in vengeance but rather through charity that I give you these trials."

I then took the liberty of asking whether the Chaplet which I recited to glorify His Name and honor the Mysteries of His life was pleasing to Him, and He answered:

"All that one does for My glory is for Me a delicious repast!"

He encouraged me to recite this Chaplet especially at those times when I found it difficult to make mental prayer.

REVELATION OF NOVEMBER 19, 1844

*Our Lord again deplores the sins of blasphemy
which continue to outrage God's Holy Name, and
He reiterates His desire for the erection of a Society
of Reparation to atone for these crimes.*

ALMOST eight months have passed since our Lord communicated Himself to my soul regarding the Work of Reparation. In the meantime He led me through a path filled with dryness, darkness and temptations. However, by the grace of God, I continued to recite the prayers of Reparation for blasphemies although I must admit that I have fallen somewhat into the snares of Satan who did everying in his power to make me grow sick of it.

Our Divine Lord now made known to me that blasphemers offend Him in a heart-rending manner, and that it was necessary to pray unceasingly to God for the favor of obtaining the establishment of the Work of Reparation. To incline God to grant this grace, we must offer to the Eternal Father the merits of our Lord and all His ardent desires to glorify the Name of His Father which always burned in His Heart while He lived on earth.

Our Lord then made me hear that mankind is unable to comprehend how enormous is the insult offered to God by blasphemy, and He explained that these sinners pierce His Heart and make of Him a second Lazarus, covered with sores.

He further told me that I, as it were, bandaged these divine sores and consoled Him in a singular manner by using my tongue to daily glorify the Holy Name of God, scorned and blasphemed by sinners, whenever I performed this exercise without seeking any gratifying consolations.

"Use every available means in your power to bring about the establishment of the Work of Reparation," our Lord told me. "For this purpose I give you all My merits that through them you may obtain this favor from My Father. Ask for this great grace in My Name, and it will be granted to you."

DECLARATION

I declare that it is I, myself, Sister Mary of St. Peter and of the Holy Family, unworthy Carmelite, who has received these Revelations regarding the Work of Reparation for blasphemy, in spite of my unworthiness, and that it is I who have written them in this tablet through obedience to my superiors. This I have done for the greater glory of God and to acquit myself of a duty of conscience, as I tremble at the sight of the mission given me by God. If our Lord's designs herein revealed are fulfilled, many souls will be saved.

I also declare that I have spoken in all truth and in the simplicity of my soul and that if it were necessary, I would be willing to attest to this by taking an oath. And now, believing it useless to keep these letters which I have copied here exactly, I will burn them.

SISTER MARY OF ST. PETER
AND OF THE HOLY FAMILY

REVELATION REPORT OF JUNE 17, 1845

Sister Mary of St. Peter explains that our Lord commanded her to speak to the Archbishop, and to ask him to establish the Work of Reparation.

I HAVE RECEIVED very little communication from our Lord regarding the Work of Reparation since November 19, 1844 until today, June 17, 1845, on which I render this report. But, Oh, how my soul suffered during that time. I could not eat, and I felt I could no longer live. God Alone knows how severe was the martyrdom through which I then passed.

Our Lord told me to address myself *in person* to the Archbishop regarding the establishment of the Work of Reparation and not to fear. He said that He would accompany me, and that He Himself would suggest what I must say to the prelate. Our Divine Saviour indeed kept His promise for I spoke to this worthy Archbishop with due respect for his high office, but yet with the simplicity of a child towards his father, and without feeling too much intimidated. The following is an account of the interview which I had with His Excellency on the subject of the Work of Reparation for blasphemy.

Having humbly asked the Archbishop to promote the establishment of the Work of Reparation so happily begun for the glory of God's Holy Name, I explained to him how strongly God urged me to work for this end.

"My child," the Archbishop answered, "I desire with all my heart to establish the Work and to give it all the public endorsement which it deserves. But this is a difficult matter. If you only knew, as I do, the obstacles! We already have much trouble trying to make people walk in the ordinary ways of piety and what would they say were I to suggest something additional? Might this not only provoke some to blaspheme anew? Present our difficulties to God, pray very much for me, and ask God to give you new revelations on the subject. If God grants you more communications make them known to me."

Then, in an effort to reassure me about my past revelations, the Archbishop said:

"My child, the revelations that you have had do not bear the stamp of delusion. On the contrary, I recognize in these communications the true mark of God. Having made some inquiries, we learned that others have had the same inspirations as you have had concerning this Work of Reparation. It already exists throughout Italy, and even here in France several dioceses are now introducing it. I desire very much that all pious souls practice this devotion, but you, my child, above all, surrender yourself to God as a victim. Offer all your penances and good works in a spirit of reparation, praying for the Church and for France. Try to stop the arm of God's justice from striking our nation. When the Lord inspires you, recite the Prayers of Reparation, but I would prefer that you should rather say only the ordinary prayers."

When I told His Excellency that I always worried and feared that perhaps at times my imagination was intermingled in these matters, he reassured me, saying:

"Be perfectly at ease on this point for as long as you open your soul in obedience to your superiors, and abandon these things to their judgment, you cannot be led astray."

Finally, on leaving, he said to me:

"I find everything in good order. Beg our Lord to enlighten me so that we can act only for the glory of God."

REVELATION OF OCTOBER 11, 1845

DESTINED IN OUR DAY TO BECOME THE FEAST OF THE
MOTHERHOOD OF THE BLESSED VIRGIN MARY, WHOSE
AIM IS TO HONOR MARY'S SINGULAR DIGNITY AS THE
MOTHER OF GOD ON WHICH ALL HER OTHER
PREROGATIVES REST

*In obedience to the Archbishop's command to pray
for further communications in regard to Reparation,
Sister Mary of St. Peter asks the Saviour for this
favor. He then reveals to her for the first time that
His Holy Face is to be the exterior object of adoration in this Work of repairing for blasphemies.*

SINCE THE TIME I had my interview with the Archbishop, I
have not experienced anything unusual on the subject of the
Work of Reparation for blasphemy although I have fulfilled
the command given me by His Excellency to pray for new
lights from our Lord on the subject of Reparation.

During this period, however, it pleased God to lead me
through another route. This Divine Spouse hid Himself from
my soul, and when I prayed He had me reflect only on my last
end. Plumbing the depth of my miserable and sinful soul, our
Lord gave me vivid lights to see the abyss of my nothingness.
I saw that I was only a shadow of a Carmelite, and that I
was indeed very much a stranger to the real thing. After
receiving these illuminations, I acknowledged my guilt and
begged our Lord to have the kindness to select another instrument, not as worthless as myself, for the accomplishment of
His designs.

After this our Lord allowed me to be tried by temptations. I felt within me only dispositions to do evil, and had our Lord not sustained me I would have fallen into many faults. I feared that in this condition my soul might lose sanctifying grace, and consequently I was in agony. "Lord," I would cry out, "hold me or I will die."

At times I was afraid to receive Holy Communion, for I had but a heart of ice to offer to my Divine Spouse. I was hardly able even to praise the Holy Name of God, as this exercise of Reparation, once so dear to me, now only produced bitterness and disgust. Yet at the very bottom of my soul it seemed to me that God still demanded of me that I be faithful to this Devotion.

Now, this morning, while I was wondering whether I dared to receive Holy Communion in this condition, I said to myself that the bread of the strong will help me to keep up my courage. So during Holy Mass, taking my crucifix and recalling that our Lord had told me that by reciting the Golden Arrow His Heart would be wounded with delights, I said the Golden Arrow ten times over. After that I resolved to receive Holy Communion in reparation for all the blasphemies perpetrated against the Divine Majesty.

I needed nothing more. The heart of my Divine Spouse was touched. How good is God, how great His mercy! After receiving Holy Communion, our Lord immediately revealed Himself to me, telling me that it was still as always His divine will that I exert myself in establishing the Work of Reparation for blasphemy in spite of the vehement efforts of the demon who filled my soul with sadness and repugnance, planning by these tactics to stop me and wishing to crush and annihilate altogether the Work of Reparation if it were at all in his power to affect this.

Immediately after that our Lord carried me in spirit to the

road leading up Calvary, and there He vividly showed me the pious deed of charity which St. Veronica performed towards Him when with her veil she wiped His Most Holy Face covered with spittle, dust, sweat and blood. Then this Divine Saviour told me that in our present age the wicked, by their blasphemies, renew all those outrages that disfigured His Holy Face on that occasion. I was enlightened to see that all the blasphemies which wicked men hurl against the Divinity, Whom they cannot reach, fall back like the spittle of the mob upon the Holy Face of our Lord, Who offered Himself a victim for sinners.

Our Lord then instructed me saying that I must imitate the courage of St. Veronica, who bravely broke through the mob of His enemies to reach Him, and that He now presented her to me as my protectress and as my model.

Following this, our Lord told me that by practicing Reparation for blasphemy, we render Him the same service as did the pious Veronica and that just as He looked with kindly eyes upon this holy woman during His passion, so would He regard with affection all those who make reparation. I could see from our Lord's attitude that He had a very tender love for St. Veronica.

Our Lord also told me that He wanted her to be particularly honored in our community, and He invited me to ask for whatever favor we wished through the service which St. Veronica rendered Him when she wiped His Holy Face, promising me that He would grant it.

I believe that our Lord also ordered me to tell the Prioress that she should make known to the Sisters of our community these considerations regarding the excellence of this devotion to the Holy Face. Our Saviour also made me understand how pleased He was that the nuns in our convent were at the present time reciting the "Golden Arrow" a certain number of times daily, thus making Reparation for blasphemy.

As for myself, our Lord made me see that He used me merely as a simple and ordinary instrument to introduce this resplendent devotion into the community, which, now being practiced by good souls, rendered Him a pleasing service. He added that if the Sisters continued to be faithful to this devotion, our convent would reap choice blessings through its means.

REVELATION OF OCTOBER 27, 1845

Being the Vigil of the Feast of St. Simon and also of St. Jude, who bearing the same name as did the traitor Judas, was frequently mistaken for that wicked betrayer, which caused St. Jude much sorrow. Undoubtedly, to prove through one exterior gesture that he was not the traitor, St. Jude decided to carry habitually a picture of Christ wherever he went. Significantly, on this Vigil our Saviour reveals to Sister Mary of St. Peter that a picture of the Holy Face should be the exterior symbol to be venerated by members in the Work of Reparation, similarly as the Sacred Heart is the exterior object representing His boundless love in the Eucharist. This revelation on the Holy Face here given is one of the most exalted conferred on the nun of Tours, at the end of which our Saviour Himself declares: "Now if there will still be those who will not recognize that this is truly My Work, it is because they close their eyes!"

SINCE OCTOBER 11, the day on which I received the first revelation on the Holy Face in connection with the Work of Reparation for blasphemy, nothing of an extraordinary nature has transpired in my soul. I believe, however, that I am constantly occupied in adoring the august and Holy Face of our Divine Saviour.

During these last days I felt inspired to petition our Lord to grant me new revelations on this Work, since the Archbishop told me during his interview to ask for them.

"You know well, my God, that it is through holy obedience that I address my request, and on the part of our Archbishop," I said to our Saviour after Holy Communion, but He did not deem it opportune to answer me. Instead, He plunged me into profound contemplation of His adorable Face.

This morning, however, as soon as I had arrived in choir for mental prayer, our Lord revealed Himself to me in His usual manner, which always happens when I least expect it. He made me see and hear what marvelous plans He had in mind by revealing to humanity the Work of Reparation, and He explained to me that the communications which He would now impart to me were an answer to my petition addressed to Him a short while before on the part of our Archbishop.

Drawing me strongly to the contemplation of His adorable Face, our Divine Saviour made me see through a ray of light issuing from His august Countenance that the Holy Face which He presented to mankind for their adoration, was indeed the mirror of those unutterable Divine Perfections comprised and contained in the Most Holy Name of God.

It is impossible for me to express in words all that I understood through this intellectual vision, unless it be by those words of the Apostle St. Paul: "The Head of Christ is God." Coming upon this text recently, I was deeply impressed by it because I recognized in these words the truth of that which was revealed to me in my vision.

I then understood by this illumination that as the Sacred Heart of Jesus is the exterior object offered for our adoration, to represent His boundless love in the most Holy Sacrament of the Altar, so in a parallel manner, in the Work of Reparation, the adorable Face of our Lord is the exterior object offered for the adoration of the members. I saw that by thus honoring and venerating this Sacred Countenance covered anew with outrages, we could atone for blasphemers who attack the

Divinity of which this Holy Face is the figure, the mirror and the expression.

By virtue of this Holy Face, offered to the Eternal Father, we can appease His anger and obtain the conversion of the wicked and of blasphemers. Therefore, such a devotion to the Holy Face can in no wise be contrary to the Work of Reparation, but it is rather a stimulus to its widespread growth.

Our Lord also made me see that the Church is His Mystical Body and that Religion is the face of that Mystical Body. Then He showed me this Face as the butt of all the enemies of His Holy Name and I saw that all blasphemers and dissenters inflicted once more the sufferings of the Passion upon our Lord's Holy Face. By this divine illumination I saw also that the impious in uttering wicked words, and in blaspheming the Holy Name of God spit in our Lord's Face, and cover it with mud. I comprehended too that all the blows which dissenters inflict upon Holy Church, attacking Religion, are a renewal of the numerous blows which our Lord's Face received in the Passion, and also that these blows were inflicted on Him by those who attempted to stamp out the Works of God.

After this vision our Lord said to me:

"I seek Veronicas to wipe and venerate My Divine Face which has but few adorers!" And then He reassured me that all persons who would apply themselves to this Work of Reparation would perform the same service in His behalf as that which the saintly Veronica had performed.

Then our Lord addressed me saying:

"To you I give My Holy Face as a recompense for the services you have performed for Me during the past two years. It is true you have actually achieved only little but your heart is filled with ardent desires. To you, therefore, I now give this Holy Face in the presence of My Eternal Father and in virtue of the Holy Ghost. Before all the angels and saints, I offer you this gift of My Holy Countenance through the hands of My Mother and those of St. Veronica who will teach you how it must be venerated."

Then our Lord added:

"By My Holy Face you will work wonders!" He made known to me that He desired to see His Holy Face offered as the exterior object of adoration to all His children who would be associated in the Work of Reparation for Blasphemy. Inviting me to make known His Holy Face from this standpoint, our Lord then declared that the gift of His adorable Countenance which He presented to me on that day was, next to the Sacraments, the greatest gift He could bestow on me.

He showed me how He had prepared me for its reception by tilling the ground of my soul with severe interior trials which I had recently endured, making me understand, however, that He never tempted His children beyond their strength.

I was further given to understand that He had appointed St. Louis, the king of France, as the protector of this Work of Reparation on account of the zeal which this saint evinced for the glory of His Holy Name, and that St. Veronica was to be its protectress because of the service of love which she had rendered Him in wiping His adorable Face on the road to Calvary.

Having finished giving me these vivid revelations on the Work of Reparation, our Lord further declared:

"Now if there will still be those who will not recognize that this is truly My Work, it is because they close their eyes!"

At the end I felt somewhat uneasy concerning the reality of this revelation on account of its great length, but our Lord reassured me saying that He had many different ways of communicating Himself to souls. He said that in my case He accommodated Himself to my meager capacity, and that by now I ought to readily recognize Him, knowing by experience

that He always communicated Himself to me in the same
sweet and pleasing manner.

REVELATION OF OCTOBER 28, 1845
THE FEAST OF THE APOSTLE ST. JUDE THADDEUS

*This communication explains that as in an earthly
kingdom money which bears the picture of the ruler
or head of a country is legal tender for purchasing
whatever one wishes, so through the precious humanity of our Lord, bearing the picture of His Face,
one can purchase all he desires from God.*

DURING EVENING PRAYER on the feast of the holy apostles,
Saints Simon and Jude, our Lord condescended to abase Himself towards my ungrateful soul by revealing Himself to me.
Since I had some difficulty in persuading myself that our Lord
had actually presented me, who am so unworthy, with the
precious gift of His Holy Face, I begged Him to grant me a
visible proof of the invisible grace, which I believed I had
received from His mercy, the previous day.

Having chosen as the subject of my meditation the betrayal
of our Lord by Judas, I was reflecting with sadness on the
shame inflicted on the Holy Face of our Saviour by the perfidi-
ous kiss of His disciple, when it seems to me our Lord invited
me to kiss most lovingly the Image of His Holy Face in a
spirit of Reparation. Having made several acts of love, I felt
that our Lord was drawing me to Himself, and obeying the
touch of grace, I saw that this Divine Saviour intended to
instruct me on the value of the gift He had bestowed on me
when He presented me with His Holy Face. Having the kindness to adapt Himself to the scant powers of my poor understanding, our Saviour suggested the following simple comparison to me:

"Just as in an earthly kingdom," He stated, "money which is stamped with the picture of the sovereign or ruling executive of the country procures whatever one desires to purchase, so likewise in the Kingdom of Heaven, you shall obtain all that you desire by offering the coin of My precious Humanity which is My adorable Face."

These divine revelations which I am forced to express in language all too feeble to convey the meaning of what I understood, have placed me beside myself with joy. Since, moreover, I experienced within me a sublime transformation, impossible to describe, I begged our Lord to instruct me and make somewhat more intelligible to my meager understanding that which I then felt, for even the faculties of my soul seemed to be suspended.

Thereupon our Lord willed that I should momentarily be transported in spirit to consider a certain piece of land adjoining the convent, for which our Prioress had previously told me to pray to our Lord, bidding me to ask Him for it. Presently it seemed to me that the Divine Saviour was beckoning me to purchase this land by offering the Holy Face, and He further assured me saying that before another year would elapse, our Community would be in possession of this land, adding that I should not in the meantime worry as to how this would be brought about.

REVELATION OF OCTOBER 30, 1845

*In this revelation our Lord imparts a most sublime
instruction, showing the position of the Holy Face
in relation to the Adorable Trinity Itself.*

REMEMBER, Oh, my soul, the holy instruction which your
Divine Spouse imparted to you today concerning His adorable
Face. Remember that this Divine Head represents the Eternal
Father Who is unbegotten, that the mouth of this Holy Face
represents the Divine Word, begotten of the Father, and that
the two eyes of this adorable Face are the symbol of the
reciprocal love of the Father and the Son, for these two eyes
possess only one light, and one identical knowledge between
them both, and they produce the one same love, which represents the Holy Ghost.

Contemplate in His locks of hair the infinite number of the
adorable perfections of the Blessed Trinity. Behold in this
majestic Head that precious portion of the Humanity of the
Saviour which is the very Image of the Oneness of God.

Now it is this adorable Saviour's Face brimming with ineffable mysteries which blasphemers cover with disgrace, renewing the bitter sufferings of His Passion, each time they
assail the Divinity, for the Holy Face is the very Image of God!

REVELATION OF NOVEMBER 5, 1845

*Our Lord further instructs Sister Mary of St. Peter
about the excellence of Devotion to the Holy Face,
saying that His Sacred Face is like a Divine Stamp,
reproducing the Image of God in souls.*

OUR DIVINE SAVIOUR told me that He has undertaken to bring
to the knowledge of men the power residing in His adorable
Face in order to restore the Image of God in those souls who
have lost it through sin. He then showed me in the Apostle
St. Peter an example of the power emanating from His Holy
Face, for being smitten with one look from the Face of Jesus,
the faithless apostle at once repented: "Jesus looked at Peter
and Peter wept bitterly."

By a divine illumination I see that this adorable Face is a
Divine Stamp which has the power of imprinting anew the
Image of God upon those souls to whom this Seal is applied.
Transported with joy at this celestial vision I am moved, there-
fore, to salute the Holy Face in these words:

"I salute You, I adore You, and I love You, Oh, adorable
Face of my beloved Jesus, as the noble Stamp of the Divinity!
Completely surrendering my soul to You, I most humbly beg
that this Seal be affixed upon us all so that the Image of God
may once more be reproduced by its imprint in our souls!"

In this Work, man is invited to make reparation for the
outrages committed against God in return for which God
promises us to restore His Image in our souls, by applying
to them the virtue of His Holy Face. What a mystery of love!
I believe that God has great plans of showing mercy to souls

by revealing to us the power of His adorable Countenance. In this priceless gift we possess an infallible means of appeasing the anger of the Eternal Father, irritated by blasphemers because whenever we beg Him to cast a look on the Face of His Divine Son, the rod falls from His hands. "Behold, Oh, God, our Protector and look on the Face of Your Christ!"

REVELATION OF JANUARY 5, 1846

VIGIL OF THE EPIPHANY

Our Lord chose the Eve of this great Feast, commemorating as it does His manifestation to the gentiles, to grant Sister Mary of St. Peter the LOFTIEST *of all His revelations on the Holy Face. In this exalted communication, the Divine Redeemer holds out blessings of unbounded hope even for those blasphemers who* OPENLY *attack Religion and the Holy Catholic Church. Referring to this class of sinners as "His poor sheep, bitten by the serpent and infected with the* MADNESS *of blasphemy," the Saviour entrusts them to Sister Mary's care, appointing her as their shepherdess. He solemnly enjoins her that "she* MUST *lead these poor sheep to graze on the pastures of the divine mysteries of His life in order that they might be* CURED, *and He bids her to brand all these poor straying sheep with the picture of His Holy Face. Later, taking the Sister to task for mistrusting somewhat the Mercy of God, and neglecting to pray sufficiently for blasphemers, the Saviour pointed to Himself as the First Model of those who entreated the Eternal Father in behalf of this class of sinners, saying: "Did I not Myself give you the example of praying for blasphemers while I was on the cross?"*

THE DIVINE MASTER made known to me that the land (adjoining our convent) which we purchased from His Heavenly Father through the offering of His Holy Face was to serve as

[165]

a symbol of the land of the living which we must buy for a large number of souls with the divine and mysterious coin of His adorable Face. This Divine Shepherd afterwards showed me a sheepfold and He said that He appointed me as its shepherdess.

Our Lord then made me understand that these, His poor sheep, had been bitten by the serpent who had infected them with the madness of blasphemy. He told me that I must lead these poor sheep to graze on the pastures of the Divine mysteries of His life in order that they might be cured, and He also said that I must shelter these sheep in the adorable wounds of His Sacred Heart and that I must brand them with the picture of His Holy Face.

However, the Divine Saviour also warned me that I would have much to suffer because this herd of blasphemers was in a special manner under the leadership of the prince of demons, that is Lucifer himself. As for the various flocks composed of other sinners, for example the immoral, the drunkards, and the avaricious, Lucifer left these sinners to be led by the other, less powerful demons according as these demons willingly chose to lead various evil-doers, but that blasphemers are Lucifer's own particular herd.

"It is he," declared the Saviour, "who makes this Work of Reparation so difficult for you. But do not fear him. St. Michael and the other holy angels will protect you. I give you My cross to use as a shepherd's crook, and through this weapon you will become formidable to the demon."

After that our Lord made me hear that it was for this very mission that He had withdrawn me from the world and called me to live in this His holy house. Fearing as always that I was being deluded, I experienced a certain uneasiness about this revelation but our Lord hastened to reassure me saying:

"Be calm! Satan has too great a fear of the cross to mark any of his works with it."

During prayer on another recent occasion, our Lord reprimanded me for neglecting to pray for the conversion of blasphemers. He showed me that I had listened to the demon and that I had allowed that wicked spirit to tempt me to mistrust the mercy of God. Then the Saviour added:

"Did I not Myself give you the example of praying for blasphemers while I was on the cross?"

After that our Saviour told me that He had great plans of showing mercy to this particular class of sinners, and that He desired to use me as an instrument for the accomplishment of these plans, in spite of my unworthiness, through the inauguration of the Work of Reparation. He further explained to me that this Work included not only reparation for what is generally called blasphemy, that is abusing the Holy Name of God, but that it also embraced reparation for all attacks against Religion and against Holy Church, since these also constitute a form of blasphemy.

REVELATION OF JANUARY 23, 1846

FEAST OF THE ESPOUSALS OF THE BLESSED VIRGIN

*Our Lord complains again that the nation is pro-
voking the justice of God, and that Sister Mary
should offer the Holy Face in reparation, or else the
guilty country will reap chastisements.*

I CANNOT restrain my tears at the thought of what our Lord
told me after I received Holy Communion this morning. The
following are the terrifying words which He spoke to me:

"The face of this nation has become unsightly in the eyes
of My Father. The people are provoking the arm of His
justice. To obtain mercy, offer therefore to the Eternal Father
the Face of His Son in which He takes His delights. Unless
this be done, the nation will experience God's just punishments. Yet the country's deliverance from these evils lies in
the Face of the Saviour. Behold here another proof of My
goodness towards this nation which repays Me with ingrati-
tude!"

Frightened I said to our Lord, "Saviour, is it really You
Who gives me these revelations?" He answered me:

"Were you able to obtain them yourself at the time of your
last Communion? I purposely abandoned you to profound
darkness during the last eight days to help you realize that it
is I Who reveal Myself to you."

I then prayed as follows:

"Eternal Father, we offer You the adorable Face of Your
Well-beloved Son, for the honor and glory of Your Holy
Name, and for the salvation of our country."

REVELATION OF MARCH 8, 1846

Our Lord in this revelation to the Sister expresses His gratitude to the Prioress of the convent for her efforts in trying to spread the Work of Reparation.

OUR LORD this morning showed me His Precious Head crowned with thorns and His adorable Face as a target at which are flung outrageous insults by the enemies of God and of the Church. Once more I heard His sad sighs. He told me that He was seeking in our convent souls who would heal the wounds inflicted on His Face by pouring over them the wine of compassion and the oil of love, which is Reparation. Then our Lord promised that if the community embraced this exercise of Reparation, He would give it a kiss of love which would be the pledge of the eternal kiss.

It seemed to me also that our Lord told me to thank the Prioress for her efforts in furthering His Work of Reparation, encouraging her to continue.

Fearing illusion, I told our Lord that it was my desire never to utter anything which might be only the simple effect of my imagination. Thereupon the Divine Saviour urged me by every means to plead His cause, and to beg that some relief be given Him in His cruel sufferings. This day was for me, therefore, one full of anguish yet I considered myself favored to be able to suffer, for our Lord made known to me that in sharing His pains, dividing them between us two, as it were, He felt greatly relieved.

I therefore beg that the Prayers of Reparation be spread among our convents since they are so pleasing to our Lord that they actually assuage His fearful grief. It had been five weeks since our Lord's last revelation and during this time I continued to make reparation, yearning for the establishment of the Work, while I peacefully occupy myself with the flocks our Lord has entrusted to my charge, so that not one of these sheep for which the Divine Master gave His life should perish.

REVELATION OF MARCH 12, 1846

In this communication our Saviour points to one of the least known among the Saints, the Good Thief, St. Dysmas, who through a last-minute public act of Reparation obtained forgiveness. He is to be a model for priests who now imitating His bold, open defense of the Saviour's cause on Calvary, must openly from the pulpit preach and defend His cause of Reparation.

OUR LORD revealed Himself to me this morning after Holy Communion and He made known to me that two persons had rendered Him a particular service during His Passion. The first of these was the pious Veronica (already mentioned), who honored His Sacred Humanity by wiping His adorable Face on the road to Calvary. The second person was the Good Thief, who, from the cross as from a pulpit, openly defended the Saviour's cause, confessing His Divinity, and glorifying Him while He was being blasphemed by the other thief and by the mob.

Our Lord made me understand that these two persons were presented to the members of the Association of Reparation as models. St. Veronica is the model for persons of her own sex who are called to serve Him, not by preaching sermons, but by wiping His Holy Face in a spirit of reparation for blasphemies through their prayers, their praises and adoration.

The Good Thief, however, who so openly and boldly defended the Saviour's cause on Calvary, is held up more especially as a model to priests who must now imitate him, and through their public preaching defend the Cause of Reparation.

After telling me this, our Saviour invited me to notice what magnificent rewards He had immediately bestowed on these two persons for their services in His behalf. To the first, that is to St. Veronica, He gave a Picture of Himself, by impressing the divine features of His Sacred Face on her veil. As for the other, that is the Good Thief (St. Dysmas), our Lord conferred upon him that very day the gift of eternal blessedness, admitting him into the Kingdom of Heaven.

Then our Lord promised me that all who defended His cause in the Work of Reparation, whether by their words, their prayers or by their writings, He would Himself defend before His Eternal Father, and that He would give them His Kingdom. Then it seemed to me that our Lord urged me to extend this promise in His Name to His priests, who through a crusade of preaching would advance the cause of Reparation.

As for His spouses who would strive to honor and wipe His Holy Face in a spirit of atoning for blasphemies, our Lord promised that at their death He would purify the face of their souls by effacing the stains of sin, and that He would restore to them their original beauty.

After that our Lord said to me:

"Write down these promises for they will make a greater impression on souls than all that you have already said regarding this Work, because these promises which speak of eternal rewards will greatly stimulate the interest of the faithful, which interest I do not condemn since I have given My life to merit the Kingdom of Heaven for sinners."

Then our Lord added:

"You will be guilty of an act of injustice if you do not make known these revelations!"

REVELATION OF MARCH 23, 1846

*In this communication our Saviour explains that it
is He Himself, and His Spouse, Holy Church, who
have given birth to this Devotion. But He also insists
that in order to live, this Work must be approved
by the Divine Authority of the Church,
that is, by Rome.*

BEHOLD a second time our Lord comes to announce additional
and magnificent promises in favor of the associates in the
Work of Reparation to the Holy Face. Our Lord said to me:
"Those who embrace this Work with true piety will not be
lost, for I Myself will defend them before My Father and I
will give them the Kingdom of Heaven. I will grant them the
grace of final perseverance." After that our Lord added:
"Do not be astonished at these promises which I make in
favor of those who devote themselves to repairing for blasphemies against God's Holy Name through the Devotion to
My Sacred Face because this Work of Reparation is the very
essence of Charity, and those who possess Charity possess life."
These are the revelations which our Saviour commanded me
to make known to my superiors. He then said that it was He
Himself, and His Spouse, Holy Church, who had given birth
to this Work of Reparation. But in order that this newly-born
Devotion should live and be properly received by the faithful,
it must be established by the Divine Authority of our Holy
Church, He told me, because without this the Work would
have no success. For this reason our Lord desires to see this
Work of Reparation built upon a solid foundation, and He

said that its purpose, as well as all its precious advantages, must be made known far and wide.

REVELATION OF OCTOBER 4, 1846

Herewith our Saviour complains of the desecra-
tion of Sundays and He urges Sister Mary to pray for
the cessation of forbidden labor on Sundays. Later
He also threatens to punish the world for these
crimes against God's Majesty not by the elements but
by the "malice of revolutionary men."

SEVERAL MONTHS have passed since I experienced anything extraordinary. Our Lord, during this time of trial, deigned however to purify my soul by great interior sufferings, as all consciousness of His Presence was withdrawn from me.

But this morning, as soon as I had received Holy Communion, He intimated to me that He wanted to keep me at His feet and I obeyed. He then made me hear these sad and frightful words:

"My justice is irritated on account of the profanations of the holy day of Sunday. I seek a victim!"

I answered, "Lord, You know that my superiors have given me permission to abandon myself into Your divine hands. Therefore do with me whatever may please You, although, I must indeed add, 'What am I, anyhow?' Oh, Lord," I further said to Him, "is it indeed You Yourself Who speaks in these revelations to me?"

Our Lord answered me:

"You shall not remain long in this doubt."

Thereupon it seemed to me that our Saviour accepted the Act of self-oblation which I had just made Him, and He told me that He would in a new way take possession of my whole being, so that in a certain manner He Himself would suffer within me, in order to appease the Divine Justice, aroused by reason of the desecration of Sunday.

After that our Lord commanded me to receive Holy Communion every Sunday for these three particular intentions:

1st. In a spirit of atoning for all forbidden works done on Sundays, which as holy days are to be sanctified.

2nd. To appease Divine Justice which was on the very verge of striking on account of the profanation of holy days.

3rd. To implore the conversion of those sinners who desecrate Sundays, and to succeed in obtaining the cessation of forbidden Sunday labor.

Following this revelation, our Lord invited me to offer His Holy Face to His Eternal Father as a means of obtaining these gifts of mercy.

Such are the communications which for more than three years I have received from our Lord, all of which are repeatedly directed towards the same end, as our Divine Saviour continues to complain of these two crimes, the profanation of Sundays and the blaspheming of God's Holy Name.

REMARK — Soon I received proof of that which He told me in this last communication when He said that He would not leave me long in doubt as to whether it was indeed He who foretold to me what chastisements of God's Justice would be felt because of the profanation of Sunday. For there occurred so frightful and so unprecedented an overflowing of the River Loire as had not been seen in centuries. The whole city of Tours was in imminent danger as terror and confusion gripped the citizens. Everywhere people acknowledged that an Omnipotent Hand was wielding the elements at will and even those persons who professed hardly any religious belief whatsoever now openly admitted that it was only through a miracle that the whole city of Tours did not perish. But the real cause that provoked God to send this punishment on the city was the profanation of Sunday, as our Lord Himself told me, yet this principal fact was and continues to be ignored.

But what filled my soul with sadness was an interior light which our Lord granted me by which I saw that God's Justice was preparing to send us still other chastisements. Our Lord communicated to me that this time He would use as the instruments of punishment, not the elements, but "the malice of revolutionary men."

REVELATION OF OCTOBER 25, 1846

Threatening further punishments to the guilty, our Saviour again urges the Sister to ask the Archbishop to establish the Work of Reparation to the Holy Face. In the meantime, He enjoins her to offer the Sacred Heart to the Eternal Father, as a Vase worthy to receive the bitter wine of God's anger.

AFTER HOLY COMMUNION our Lord told me that the cup of Divine Justice had been only partly poured out upon us as yet and I was then shown still other punishments which Divine Justice was preparing to send down to earth. At the sight of these I said to our Lord:

"Oh, sweet Jesus, if I could only drink what remains in that cup so that my brethren could be spared!"

Our Lord answering me said that He accepted my good will in this matter but that I was not able to drink the full cup, and that He Himself must drain it because He alone is able to do this.

The Divine Saviour seeing my disappointment, beckoned me to enter into His Sacred Heart. He then told me that in His excessive mercy He had given me this Heart as a Vase which alone was worthy of being presented to His Eternal Father to receive the bitter wine of His anger. Then He showed me that by passing through this Holy Channel, the bitter wine of God's anger would be changed for us into the sweet wine of His Mercy. But that since the rights of justice cannot be entirely disregarded, if I may so express myself, our Lord desires to make an alliance between His justice and His mercy, and for this end He now asks that the Work of Reparation be established. Oh, yes, our Lord will most assuredly disarm the anger of God, His Father, by offering Him from us this Reparative Work!

The following is a prayer which our Lord on this occasion dictated to me and which I now repeat continually:

"Eternal Father, look upon the Sacred Heart of Jesus which I offer to You as a Vase that it might receive the wine of Your Justice, and in passing through this Holy Channel that it may be changed for us into the Wine of Your Mercy!"

I was commanded by our Lord once more to ask His Excellency, the Archbishop, to establish this Work of Reparation. I feel that my conscience will be at peace only after I will have deposited all that appertains to this Work at the feet of the Archbishop, for I understand that this mission has been entrusted to me by our Lord.

REMARK — It was not long before we realized the truth of this communication (namely that Divine Justice was preparing to send us another kind of punishment, and that this time it would not be through the elements but through the malice of revolutionary men). Soon after this the city of Tours shook with the shocking news of a conspiracy by the Communists to seize the city government and make themselves its masters. Providentially, the bloody project of these revolutionary men was discovered in time, and although the people of the whole city were in imminent danger, yet they escaped unharmed. Without our Lord's help we would have all been lost.

REVELATION OF NOVEMBER 18, 1846

*In this exquisite communication, our Lord sur-
renders all His merits to Sister Mary of St. Peter, as
He tells her to pay with them the debts incurred by
the sins of the nation. He encourages her zeal by disclosing to her that the Work of Reparation will
ultimately be established.*

OUR LORD continues to press me urgently to pray and to
suffer for our country. He said to me:

"Just as I have taken on myself the sins of the whole world,
so I now desire that you assume those of your nation. I Myself
will suffer in you in order to appease the anger of My Father
and I will give you all My merits by which you can pay the
debts incurred by the sins of your country."

I accepted our Lord's proposal and then it was that I beheld
myself as though covered with all the sins of the nation and I
begged God's forgiveness for these sins with the same shame
as though I had committed these crimes myself.

On another day when our Lord had insisted again that I
make reparation for our whole country, I hesitated, hardly
daring to believe that He could wish to make use of so common an instrument as myself for so great a task. He then said
to me by way of comparison:

"As in the order of My Providence, in temporal affairs, I
give a particular ruler to a particular nation to be its sovereign,
cannot I also, in the order of grace, assign a particular country
to the care of a special individual in order that she should take
charge of that country's spiritual welfare? That is the reason

why I now assign this particular nation to your special care and I urge you to pray and to sacrifice yourself in its behalf."

After that our Lord declared:

"I again give you My Sacred Head so that you may offer it to My Father to appease His justice. Oh, if you but knew the power and the virtue that reside therein! And the reason why My Head possesses this power and virtue is because I have taken upon My Head all the sins of mankind so that My Members may be spared. Therefore, offer My Face to My Eternal Father for this is the means by which to appease Him."

He then added:

"I desire this Work of Reparation. Although the fruits which you bear have not yet ripened be assured that finally the time will come when the Work shall be established."

REVELATION OF NOVEMBER 22, 1846

*Placing no bounds to the efficacy of the Devotion
to the Holy Face, our Saviour informs Sister Mary
of St. Peter that the treasure of His Face is of such
tremendous value that through It* ALL
matters can be settled!

HERE IS the substance of a new revelation which our Lord
gave me relative to the Holy Face:

"My daughter," He said, "I take you today for my steward-
ess. I place My Holy Face in your hands that you may offer it
unceasingly to My Father for the salvation of your country.
Turn this divine gift to good profit, for the treasure of My
Holy Face in itself possesses such tremendous value that
through It all the affairs of My household can readily be settled. Through this Holy Face you will obtain the conversion
of many sinners. Nothing that you ask in virtue of the Holy
Face will be refused you. Oh, if you only knew how pleasing
is the sight of My Face to My Father!"

REVELATION OF DECEMBER 21, 1846

Explaining to Sister Mary that similarly as the rich would be compelled to render an account to God showing whether they helped the poor with their surplus wealth, so would Religious, and particularly Carmelites, be required to answer how they utilized the spiritual riches at their disposal to help poor sinners. To encourage Sister Mary to persevere in her prayers which she recited 100 times each day, offering the Holy Face to the Eternal Father for the salvation of the country, our Saviour showed her these prayers as a mysterious Wall protecting the nation from the darts of Divine Justice.

It is hardly in my power to explain what transpired within me during the last fifteen days as our Lord poured out upon this my miserable soul torrents of precious graces. This Divine Director of my soul spoke to me as follows:

"My daughter, surrender yourself more completely to My guidance, and endeavor to have more simplicity for I Myself want to impart to you true nourishment for your soul. Your repeated fears about being deceived, as also your uneasiness and frequent disquietude, prevent Me from acting in you as freely as I desire."

I then confessed that to be my fault and our Lord hastened to wield a new power over me by disclosing to me several wonderful secrets of His infinite mercy.

Another day our Lord showed me the multitude of souls that were continually falling into hell, and He invited me in a most touching manner to help these poor sinners. He pointed out to me in particular that Religious have a most strict obligation towards these poor, blind souls who precipitate themselves into the eternal abyss, and that if other charitable souls would ask grace and mercy for these blinded ones, God's mercifulness would open their eyes.

Our Saviour also said to me that if He would require rich people to render Him a strict account to show whether they really helped the poor with the surplus temporal wealth He had entrusted to them, with what greater severity would He not demand an account from a Carmelite, who as a Religious was rich to overflowing with the wealth of her celestial Spouse. He said that such a Religious would be compelled to show what use she had made of these treasures to bring about the salvation of other immortal souls. Our Lord added:

"My daughter, I give you My Face and My Heart. I give you My Blood, and I open to you My Wounds. Draw from these and pour out their spiritual riches on others. Buy without money! My Blood is the price for souls! Oh, how painful it is to My Heart to see remedies, which have cost Me so dearly, scorned! Ask of My Father as many souls as was the number of the drops of Blood that I shed in My Passion!"

On another day our Lord showed me His Holy Cross, saying that He had given birth to all His children on this bed of pain. Then He made me understand that in carrying the Cross for love of Him, and through prayers, I would obtain eternal life for those who were dead to grace, and whose resurrection He desired so ardently. Oh, what yearnings I see in the Heart of Jesus for the salvation of sinners!

On still another day our Lord placed my soul at the brink of Eternity, or rather at the gate of Time, that I might help sinners during their last agony in that dreadful journey from Time to Eternity.

Finally, our Lord gave me a vision in which I saw a mysterious wall protecting our nation from the darts of Divine Justice. Our Lord told me that this wall which reached to Heaven was the special daily devotion which I offered for the needs of our nation, undoubtedly joined to the prayers and merits which many pious souls offered to God for the same intention. This devotion consists in reciting one hundred times each day a prayer wherein the Holy Face of our Lord is offered to His Eternal Father in honor of all the Sacred Mysteries of the Saviour's life and death to implore the salvation of our country. Our Lord told me that He gave me this vision to encourage me to persevere.

REVELATION OF JANUARY 10, 1847

Scaling new heights of spiritual endeavor, rarely encountered in the lives of even the greatest saints, this revelation indicates the unique position of Sister Mary of St. Peter. Our Lord, having on December 21, mystically placed this rare soul at the brink of Eternity, to help dying sinners, today's communication reveals that for three weeks this chosen nun continually accompanied the Blessed Virgin in spirit, rendering assistance to the dying.

DURING the last three weeks our Lord has continually kept me engaged in giving spiritual assistance to the dying. Our Lord made known to me that He had assigned me to the Blessed Virgin as her little servant, and in this role I, in spirit, accompany her to help the travelers from Time to Eternity.

It seems to me that our Lord told me that I have not quite three years left to live. Being now thirty years of age, I shall, in imitation of our Lord, employ my remaining years pursuing His sheep that are lost. Oh, blindness of men that runs after the perishable riches of this earth whose aggregate value could not even purchase a single soul! Yet in the meantime it scorns all that our Redeemer has done for us, which treasure suffices to purchase millions of souls if we but present these His merits at the bank of Divine Mercy.

REVELATION OF JANUARY 21, 1847

Our Saviour analyzes the logical connection that exists between the NAME *and the* FACE *of a person, by drawing a striking comparison. In a sublime conclusion that reaches a climax in all these revelations, we are made to see, as never before, the inseparable connection in honoring the unutterable Name of God, through the "Golden Arrow" and in venerating the Holy Face of Christ.*

OUR LORD led me to make a short interior retreat, during which I was no longer obliged to exert myself in order to pray, for I felt myself in the hands of our Lord, Who Himself stirred within me feelings of compassion and most tender longing to love Him. Then it was that I heard our Saviour complain sighing that His love in the Most Blessed Sacrament of the Altar was not appreciated because of the lack of faith among Christians. In order that I may keep Him company in His loneliness, He has delightfully chained my heart and mind to remain at His feet before the Altar, where I continually adore His Most Holy Face hidden under the veil of the Eucharist.

Yes, it is through this august Sacrament that Jesus, our Saviour, desires to impart to souls the rare virtue emanating from His most Holy Face, for indeed there in the Blessed Sacrament of the Altar His adorable Face is more dazzling than the sun. He then once more promised me to imprint His Divine likeness upon the souls of those who honor the features of His Face.

[187]

Then our Lord showed me by means of a comparison, both simple and appropriate, the special connection existing between His Holy Name and His Holy Face. He made me understand that whereas merit accruing from noble actions is always attached to persons themselves, yet the glory which accompanies this merit is always attached to the names of these persons. In short, I saw that the merit or demerit of any person is always attached to his name, so that each time the name of a person is mentioned, it recalls either the glory of that person or his ignominy.

Because the most Holy Name of God expresses the Divinity, and all the perfections of the Creator, it follows from this that blasphemers of this Sacred Name attack God Himself. Recalling the words of our Lord Who said, "I am in the Father and the Father is in Me," we must realize that since Jesus through His Incarnation became capable of suffering, it is He Who endures in His Adorable Face the insults offered to the Name of God, His Father, by blasphemers. I then saw that the impious through their blasphemies attack His Adorable Face, and that the Faithful glorify this Holy Face by the praises they confer on the Holy Name of God.

After that our Lord explained to me that there is always something mystifying in the facial expression of an honorable man who has been maligned. Yes, I see that a close and inexpressible relation exists between the face and the name of such a person, for our Lord showed it to me as follows. Let us take the example of one particular man, who for his outstanding deeds of merit had earned for himself a distinguished name, but look at this man while he is in the presence of his enemies. Although they do not bruise him physically by laying their hands on him, yet by uttering their slanderous accusations and sarcastic remarks against him, instead of offering titles of honor which are justly his due, they indeed injure him most painfully.

Now take notice what passes over the face of this injured man as he is being thus mistreated! Is it not evident to you that all the outrageously wicked words coming from the lips of his enemies have struck this man direct blows on his face? His whole facial expression undergoes a painful change as the insults flung at him become reflected in every line of his features which tell all too clearly that he is enduring real torments.

Look closely at the way this man's face turns red, which is only natural since he is burning with shame and confusion. Feeling cheap and disgraced, he suffers more cruelly from this embarrassment covering his face than he would suffer from various other pains that might be inflicted on different parts of his body. Well, this is but a faint picture of what the adorable Face of our Saviour endures when it is outraged by the blasphemies of the wicked.

After that our Lord made me visualize this same man in the presence of his friends, who, hearing of the insults to which he had been subjected by his enemies, at once gather around him that they might undo the wrongs he was made to endure. Joining in one voice they all begin to treat him with the dignity which he deserves, speaking highly and openly of his achievements, recommending his great deeds, and rendering honor to his distinguished name as they address him by his special titles.

Now watch the face of this man as it begins to take on an expression of sweetness, which reflects his appreciation of the praise and honor accorded to him. Soon happiness is seen resting on his brow, as momentarily it spreads over his whole face, making it radiant with contentment. Observe the joy sparkling in his eyes, and finally a blissful smile parts his lips, for behold, the entire face of this man has become transformed.

In short, the faithful friends of this man have not only wiped away the burning shame on his face, outraged by the insults of his enemies, but by their unanimous praises, they have given him so full a measure of honor that it by far surpassed the former shame he endured in his countenance. And that is precisely what the friends of our Lord Jesus Christ actually do for Him by the Work of Reparation. The honor which they give to His Name is seen reflected in His brow and in His facial expression, but especially is the Holy Face in the Blessed Sacrament made radiant with joy by means of Reparation.

I comprehend that as blasphemers cruelly afflict the Holy Face, so those who make Reparation delight and glorify It. But what I see as I never saw before is the striking connection between a person's face and his name, for the face reflects indeed either his honor or his dishonor.

REVELATION OF FEBRUARY 2, 1847

FEAST OF THE PURIFICATION

*Significantly our Saviour chose the Feast of the
Blessed Virgin's Purification to teach Sister Mary of
St. Peter how to purify her soul in imitation of the
Mother of God. Heretofore our Lord's revelations
stressed overwhelmingly only doctrinal and spiritual
verities. Today, however, the Saviour speaks to her
plainly about attending to the ordinary matter of
labor. In one sublime stroke of divine wisdom, our
Lord settles for all concerned the important and
excellent place which honest work well done holds
in the life of a Christian, without which there
is no true virtuous living.*

SINCE I felt myself growing considerably weaker for some time,
I asked the Mother Prioress to appoint another sister who
would share with me the work of the office of portress, feeling
no longer able to do this work alone on account of my health.
But the Prioress, refusing me this, said that perhaps it was my
laziness and self-love that prompted me to ask for assistance.
She also told me to ask our Lord to restore me my strength so
that at the end of fifteen days I could resume all my duties.
While I accepted this order respectfully, I must confess that I
was sadly disappointed at finding our Prioress on this occasion
lacking her ordinary sympathy, and then the demon, too, began
to tempt me.

Going to our Lord, I opened my heart to Him, shedding
many tears, as I told Him that the office of portress was for me

a continual martyrdom, because it incessantly drew me away from His presence. Yet as an act of obedience to the Prioress, I asked Him, nevertheless, to restore my health to me so that I could fulfill all my duties as I was told to do.

The following morning after Holy Communion our Lord said to me:

"My daughter, is it not true that you find very much pleasure in solitude? And furthermore, was not every day a feast-day for you during those first years you spent in the cloister, when you were given no exterior work to perform?"

"Yes, Lord," I answered.

"Well, then, my daughter, learn now that every Religious should be a living crucifix. If you did not have all these worries, how would you be able to save those souls that I have placed in your hands? To prove that it is my desire that you should be the portress, and to show you that it is I Myself Who through your superior's lips have refused you a second turn-Sister to share your work, I now will that you be cured instantly! Be very happy because for all your labors I will repay you by giving you souls."

I can say with certainty that our Lord has, indeed, granted me a complete cure, for I am able to perform all my duties as I did before I became sick.

Again revealing Himself to me later, He declared:

"I want you to imitate My industriousness. I came to earth not to be served but to serve!" and then He added:

"During a time of scarcity, when the price of bread is very high, would not the father of a family deserve the reproaches of his wife and children, if being able to work the whole day, he labored only half the day because of his laziness? Surely, working only part time the man would never be able to earn sufficient money to buy the provisions necessary for the life of his family. Well, my daughter, apply this lesson to yourself.

You, too, have children to nourish, as I have already told you, and make no mistake about it. It is essential that you earn sufficient bread for them, and to achieve this they need your entire day's labor. Therefore do not open yourself through laziness to risk hearing these souls reproach you on Judgment Day."

On still another occasion our Lord instructed me on the need of conscientiously laboring to fulfill all the work assigned, as follows:

"My daughter, you at times complain that you cannot live a life of solitude because of your many occupations, but tell me, do you know what a solitary soul really is? Behold, a soul in solitude is one that has become mistress of her passions. Therefore, such a soul continually sacrifices her self-will and in obediently attending to the various occupations imposed on her, by reason of her office, she lives the life of a true solitary, and in a certain way begins to share in the very solitude of God Himself, by living according to His Holy Will." Then our Lord added:

"And on the contrary, although a soul is sheltered in the stillness of a retreat, yet she does not deserve to be called a soul in solitude if she is distracted by the noise of her own passions and seeks self-satisfaction in doing her own will. Know and remember, therefore, that self-will is the nurse of the passions."

REVELATION OF MARCH 2, 1847

*Our Lord praises Sister Mary of St. Peter for mak-
ing a good retreat by which she discovered many
faults within her soul. Then our Saviour deplored the
lack of meditation by many in the world, saying that
because they do not seriously think over the condition
of their souls, they never learn how full
of sins they are.*

FOR THE PAST fifteen days our Lord has not communicated
anything special to me. During these days, however, I en-
deavored to reform the innermost depths of my soul, and
humbling myself at the sight of my many failures, I made
a confession of my faults yesterday, and this morning approached our Lord in Holy Communion. Wanting to abase
myself before Him, I contemplated Him surrounded with great
majesty and splendor, but He, addressing me, said:

"My daughter, I prefer rather that you consider Me covered
with wounds because sinners continually inflict them upon Me."

At that instant I had a vision of our Lord in this sad state.

"My daughter, come close and let Me confide in you." Then
this Divine Saviour spoke the following lamenting words
which broke my heart and made me shed many tears:

"I am not known, I am not loved, and My Commandments
are scorned." Then He added the following words which actually made me tremble:

"Sinners are snatched from this world and they are swept
into hell like the dust that is carried away by the fury of a
tornado. Have pity on your brothers and pray for them! With

the veil of your tender love wipe the Blood which flows from My wounds. Love Me and be assured that when you raise your heart to Me in love, I will accept it from you and keep it in security."

After that our Lord told me that He was pleased with my retreat during which I discovered so many faults within my heart and He said:

"Think, My daughter, how much your recent meditations helped you find in your soul many defects, and consider on the other hand the many unhappy people who never meditate on these truths. Labor very hard both for yourself and for them. Be to these souls like a mother who will never eat unless she shares her food with her children."

REVELATION OF MARCH 7, 1847

*Our Lord joyously announces to Sister Mary that
the hour is near when the Work of Reparation to
the Holy Face will be established, calling it the
"most beautiful work under the sun." When the
Sister still worries somewhat about certain obstacles,
He assures her that those obstacles were only "the
falling mist of the early dawn ushering in
a beautiful day."*

FOR SEVERAL MONTHS now our Lord had led me in various ways to work for the salvation of souls. But today I
heard the voice of our Lord calling me anew to the task of
making Reparation for blasphemies. This is the third time that
He has repeated His invitation to me to work for this end. I
have great confidence that this Work will be established
because some time ago our Lord Himself assured me of this. For
that reason therefore I would never abandon my hope in Him
Who is Omnipotent, even though I saw both the earth and
hell itself opposing this Work. In fact, our Lord confided to
me that He would allow the demon to cross His works to test
the fidelity of His servants.

And so today our Lord gave me the following promise:

"Rejoice, My daughter, because the hour approaches when
the most beautiful Work under the sun will be born. Offer
My Sacred Heart to the Eternal Father to obtain it."

But as I reflected on the obstacles that still stood in the way
and wondered about them, our Lord said to me:

[196]

"That is only the falling mist of the early dawn ushering in a beautiful day!"

Our Lord then urged me to surrender myself anew into His hands to suffer interiorly and exteriorly whatever He willed, in order that His plans in this Work could be accomplished, reminding me that I was but a weak tool in His hands, which He wielded as He willed. This is indeed so because I can labor at this Work only through a special grace as He wills and whenever He wills. During the past several months, for instance, I did not attend to the Work of Reparation — not from indifference but because our Lord drew me to other matters. At present, however, I feel myself under the special influence of His grace which urges me to apply myself to this work.

REVELATION OF MARCH 14, 1847

In this communication COMMUNISTS *are openly designated by our Lord as a group secretly working to advance diabolical plots and anti-Christian principles in order to inflame all society. To stop them by obtaining God's mercy, our Lord orders Sister Mary personally to ask the Archbishop, in the Name of the Saviour, to inaugurate Holy Face Devotion.*

TODAY after Holy Communion our Lord told me that the disaster caused by the flood with which we had been recently struck was only a forerunner of other punishments which Divine Justice is preparing for us if we do not appease the anger of God. He showed me the sins of blasphemy and profanation of Sunday under the symbols of two pumps, with which men guilty of these crimes are drawing the waters of God's wrath on our country, and which is in danger of being submerged if the Work of Reparation, which He has given us in His mercy as a means of deliverance, be not established.

After that our Lord told me that the Society known as the Communists had so far made only one outbreak, but that they were working secretly to advance their schemes. Then He added:

"Oh, if you only knew their secret and diabolical plots and their anti-Christian principles! They are waiting for a favorable day in order to inflame the whole country. To obtain mercy, ask therefore that this Work of Reparation be established by addressing yourself to him who through the bounden duty of his office can establish it."

"But, my Divine Master," I answered, "my superiors have already asked the Archbishop for this."

"That is not sufficient," our Lord replied. "It is you that I have chosen as the instrument and it is you who must ask for the Work to be established in My Name and on My Part."

I now beg to be told by the Prioress whether or not I am obliged to write to the Archbishop to acquaint him with this revelation for I believe I have twice received a divine command to do so.

REVELATION OF MARCH 19, 1847

FEAST OF ST. JOSEPH, PATRON OF THE UNIVERSAL CHURCH

*On this day our Saviour discloses His FULL plans
for the Work of Reparation. He calls on Sister Mary
of St. Peter to make it known that He desires this
Devotion to be approved by a Brief from Rome itself, so that it will never perish, and declares that
He created her for this Work.*

AFTER Holy Communion this morning I told our Lord that I
have been counseled by the Prioress not to write to the Archbishop on account of the many occupations which already claim
his attention. Here is what our Lord had the goodness to
answer me in regard to this matter:

"My daughter, I have a great love for obedience. Submit
to them, therefore, so that seeing you always so obedient to
your superiors in everything that I communicate to you, they
will be able to recognize the spirit by which you are led.
Nevertheless, it is My Will that these revelations which I have
given you be made known to your highest superior."

Then I said, "My Divine Master, permit me to ask You with
all the simplicity of a child to explain what You mean when
You command me to ask the Archbishop for the erection of
the Work of Reparation for You know that he has already
somewhat aided this Work by giving it his approval to a
certain extent." To this our Lord replied:

"If this Work of Reparation is not established on a solid
foundation it will never be secure. By this I mean that if it

does not have its own Brief it will only languish and wind up by perishing. This Work therefore cannot be truly established without the formality of a Brief. But on the other hand, if the Work is launched by first asking for a Brief, it will soon spread and be extended through all the cities of the nation. Now it is only proper that he who has first put his hand to the Work should bring it to a successful finish."

I then asked, "Is it really true, my Divine Master, that You told me the other day to ask His Excellency for this Work in Your Name and on Your part, for I am always afraid of being mistaken?"

Our Lord answered me saying that I can be absolutely certain of this, as He urged me to notice that this Work occupied my mind only when He Himself inspired it which is certainly the case. He then declared that He would explain to me by means of a comparison to what extent He had taken hold of my soul.

Showing me a bow and arrow which He said was the symbol of my soul in His hands, He told me to notice the special angle at which He held the bow, aiming the arrow at some particular target, as He chose for the successful accomplishment of His plans. Then He added:

"It is to use you as the instrument in My plans for this Work of Reparation that I have created you. But be consoled, for I shall not leave you long upon the earth after this Work is established, and My Mercy will then compensate you for all your little labors."

REVELATION OF MARCH 29, 1847

The Saviour enjoins Sister Mary through her prayers and the instruments of His Passion to make war on the Communists who are the enemies of the Church and her Christ. He tells her that whereas the weapons of the enemy inflict death, the weapons of His Passion restore life. This revelation strikes an unprecedented peak stressing the militancy of the Church on earth, as it demonstrates the power of the individual soul to forge her WILL against the powers of evil through prayer. It must be so for, after all, the battle real and actual which goes on between the Church and hell is not a battle of guns and mobilized divisions in uniform, for Satan has none of these at his disposal, but he employs only his formidable WILL of evil to spread disaster. Coping with this force, the Church's militant members forge their WILLS of good, through Christ, to defeat the powers of the infernal regions.

TODAY after Holy Communion our Lord gave me a new mission, one which ought to frighten me, yet since I know I am nothing but a weak instrument in His hands, I am perfectly at peace.

Our Lord commanded me to make war on the Communists because He said they were the enemies of the Church and of her Christ. He told me also that most of these wolfish men who are now Communists had been born in the Church whose

[202]

bitter enemies they now openly declare themse
our Saviour added:

"I have already told you that I hold you in 1
arrow. I now want to hurl this arrow against M., enemies. To
arm you for the battle ahead, I give you the weapons of My
Passion, that is My Cross which these enemies dread, and
also the other instruments of My tortures. Go forward to meet
these foes with the artlessness of a child, and the bravery of a
courageous soldier. Receive for this mission the benediction of
the Father, of the Son, and of the Holy Ghost."

Having been favored with this communication, I frequently
call on the Blessed Virgin to be the depositary of these sacred
weapons which her Divine Son gave me since she is called the
Tower of David on which hang a thousand bucklers.

Since our Saviour continued to grant me further lights on
this subject I now said to Him, "Lord, give me a skillful hand,
and train me to use well these weapons which You have entrusted to me for the combat." To this our Lord answered:

"The weapons of My enemies inflict death but My weapons
give life."

The following is the prayer I frequently recite to fulfill the
mission entrusted to me:

"Eternal Father, I offer You the Cross of our Lord Jesus
Christ and all the other instruments of His Holy Passion, that
You may put division in the camp of Your enemies, for as
Your Beloved Son has said, 'A kingdom divided against itself
shall fall.' "

REVELATION OF APRIL 1, 1847

*In addition to the instruments of Christ's Passion
serving as true weapons in the war with Communists,
Sister Mary is told to have recourse to the Holy
Name of God, and that of the Blessed Virgin Mary,
which are so terrifying to the demons, and that these
Holy Names will serve her as "ammunition."*

OUR LORD continues still to charge me with the mission of
making war on the Communists. He supplies me with grace
and light for the battle. The instruments of His passion serve
me as weapons of war, while the Holy Name of God which is
so terrifying to the demons, as also that of the Blessed Virgin
Mary, serve me as ammunition.

To further rouse me to this battle against God's enemies,
whom I understand through a special light to be, indeed,
formidable, our Lord said to me:

"When a soldier knows that the reason for the war to which
he is called to fight is an injury done against his ruler, he
burns with indignation to avenge this insult, and therefore
arms himself fearlessly for the encounter. Think now, My
daughter, of the outrages inflicted on Me by this Society of
Communists. They are the ones who have dragged Me from
my tabernacles, and desecrated My sanctuaries. These Communists have also dared to lay their hands on the priests of
the Lord, but all their plotting is in vain, because their schemes
will not succeed!

"Have they not committed the crime of Judas? They have
sold Me for money! This information must not remain fruit-

less in you because I am giving you these facts in order to fire you with new enthusiasm to carry on the fight. Act in a spirit of simplicity because if you will indulge in too much human reasoning, you will not be an adequate tool in My hands. Think rather of the glory that will be offered Me by the whole heavenly court for having conquered such formidable enemies with such a puny instrument!"

REVELATION OF APRIL 6, 1847

Sister Mary of St. Peter is encouraged by our Lord
to continue her valiant battle against Communism
and she is promised the reward of Heaven itself for
her faithful conduct in this war.

I HAVE entered the arena to battle with the enemies of God, and since I am engaged in this war under the banner of obedience, if I may so express myself, my soul is at peace. Fighting under this banner I feel safe, and I no longer fear the demon. Our Lord has given me the grace to launch an offensive warfare.

Today, after Holy Communion, He inspired me to be brave in the encounter, promising me that as a reward for my faithful conduct in these battles, He would give me a Cross of Honor, which would have the power of opening Heaven to me. He also promised me the gold of charity, by which I understood that I would be granted all the graces needed to triumph patiently and lovingly over any obstacles that would come my way.

Having fought the enemies of God during these past three solemn feast days,* and that with all my strength, I must explain that since I have uttered many imprecations against them, I am now somewhat saddened for having done so. I well know that the holy King David has done as much, as for example in his Psalm 108,† yet I am not certain whether the same course

---

* The three days of Holy Week.

† They have spoken against me with a lying tongue; and they have attacked me without cause. Let these my accusers be covered with shame and let them be wrapt with the mantle of their own confusion. From PSALM : 108.

[206]

is allowed me. Nevertheless, everything that I said during prayer was inspired by our Lord, and should it turn out that I have been mistaken, I will, of course, do this no more. The following is the formula of my militant procedure:

I begin by placing my soul in our Lord's hands, after which I beg Him to use my soul as He would a bow, urging Him to bend it so that the arrows would fly directly towards his enemies.

After doing this I proceed to enter the battlefield, fortified with the Cross and the other instruments of our Lord's tortures as my weapons of war, leveling their infinite conquering power against the military entrenchments of the enemy, in the way He has taught me. Then I say:

"May God arise and let His enemies be scattered and let all those who hate Him flee before His Face!

"May the thrice Holy Name of God overthrow all their plans!

"May the Holy Name of the Living God split them up by disagreements!

"May the terrible Name of the God of Eternity stamp out all their godlessness!"

Repeating other similar ejaculations, I continued to level these rounds of ammunition at God's enemies, and after I have beaten them down I add:

"Lord, I do not desire the death of the sinner, but I want him to be converted and to live. 'Father, forgive them for they know not what they do.'"

Feeling disturbed about uttering these imprecations, I sometimes worry but I must make it clear that never do I have the intention to wish evil to the enemy. I desire only to oppose their wickedness and their passions. In short, what I want is to kill not them but the "evil spirit" within them.

Such is the spiritual exercise which I perform without any

mental effort and with great ease, because I simply allow myself to be led by the grace given me, but I fully believe that there is someone very anxious to alarm me, this being the general of the opposing side, the devil.

SISTER MARY OF ST. PETER
AND OF THE HOLY FAMILY

PART III

APPENDIX

ABOUT SIX MONTHS had elapsed during which time Sister Mary of St. Peter was continually showered with unusual graces, being particularly enlightened on the Mystery of the Incarnate Word, when suddenly our Lord once more called her to work anew for the establishment of the Work of Reparation. Foretelling a disaster that was soon to befall the nation, the Saviour spoke to His emissary as follows:

"Imagine what will be the state of things in this country when soon my powerful arm will shake this throne and overthrow him who is now seated thereon."

During the following week, on December 2, 1847, the call she had was more urgent than ever as our Lord, appearing to her covered with wounds, spoke to her as follows:

"The executioners crucified Me on Friday but Christians crucify Me on Sunday. Ask then in My Name the establishment of the Work of Reparation in the Diocese of Tours, in order that My friends may embalm My wounds by their prayers and their acts of sacrifice, and thus obtain mercy for the guilty. My daughter, the storm is already rumbling but I shall keep My promise, if My wishes regarding the Reparation be respected and acted upon. Speak with humility, but at the same time with a holy freedom."

Sister Mary's revelation was promptly relayed to the Archbishop. However, when a full month passed by and there was yet no action by the diocesan authorities to arrange for a personal interview with the Carmelite, she was favored on January 4, 1848 with an extraordinary revelation which she reported as follows:

"Our holy Mother St. Teresa has appeared to me in the interior of my soul and told me that she was especially depu-

by God to fight those who were stopping the Work of Reparation. She also said that the demon was doing his utmost to
prevent the Devotion from spreading. She then made known
to me that in spite of all the opposition hurled against it, the
Work of Reparation through the Holy Face Devotion will one
day be the honor of the Order of Carmel, and she assured me,
moreover, that the Devotion is in every way conformable to
the spirit of the Carmelite vocation whose sole aim is the
glory of God and the needs of the Church. For that reason she
urged me to devote myself to it with unremitting fervor.
Finally, it was revealed to me that in addition to being designated by God as the powerful protectress of the Work of
Reparation, our holy Mother St. Teresa was assigned to me as
a consoler in my various trials. Since then I have felt my soul
closely united to this great Saint who is a model of zeal for the
glory of the Most High."

The following month, on February 13, 1848, our Lord
revealed to Sister Mary that the rumbling storm about which
He warned her was close at hand.

"During my evening prayer," she wrote in her report to the
Prioress, "our Lord made known to me that terrible woes
were impending, and He said: 'Pray, pray, for the Church is
threatened by a fearful tempest!' The Saviour made me understand that His justice was greatly irritated against mankind for
its sins but particularly for those that directly outrage the
Majesty of God — that is, Communism, Atheism, cursing, and
the desecration of Sundays.

A week later, the Sister writes again:

"On Sunday, February 20, having offered Holy Communion
e outrages against the Divine Majesty, it
my soul by an interior light that the crisis
d these words: 'The Lord has strung His
it to discharge His arrows!' Realizing how

shamefully God had been outraged, I could no longer remain neutral, as it were, and so entering into His designs of justice, I answered, 'Strike, O, Lord!' I longed for God's honor to be vindicated. Praying God to strike as a Father and not as an angry judge I saw that His stroke would not be a mortal stroke. I comprehended that this scandal, if I may so express myself, must of necessity come to pass. For more than four years had the arm of the Lord been raised over our guilty heads."

Almost immediately following this communication, news of a serious revolution in Paris shook the very foundations of the French government and all of Europe. King Louis Philippe, who after eighteen years felt himself securely established as monarch of France, was forced to flee with his family into exile.

Learning of this, Sister Mary of St. Peter redoubled her zeal in making reparation so that she now prayed almost incessantly. On February 26, she writes:

"The Lord has told me that in consequence of the initial efforts made to establish somewhat the Work of Reparation, our country which was to be almost entirely destroyed by the darts of His justice, would now only be partly punished by the terrible flames of His anger. Oh, how I long to entreat all the Bishops to establish the Work of the Reparation in their dioceses."

Unfortunately, this apostle of the Holy Face who so longed to entreat all Ordinaries to erect Confraternities of Reparation was to be so thwarted in her mission, that she was prevented from addressing personally even her own diocesan superior. Although three months elapsed since she was last enjoined by the Saviour to ask in His Name for the establishment of the Work of Reparation in the Diocese of Tours, no steps towards arranging an interview were forthcoming.

On March 3, however, our Lord communicated to her a

final ultimatum. It assumed the nature of a positive command, that either the Ordinary of the diocese, or his Secretary, come without further delay to the Carmelite convent where Sister Mary of St. Peter was to tell them personally what had been revealed to her during the past four and a half years regarding the Work of Reparation to the Holy Face.

"Our Lord has just made known to me after Holy Communion," wrote Sister Mary, "that it is His express will that I speak to His Excellency or to his Secretary and that I acquaint either of them with the communications which I have received from the Saviour during the last four years and a half. Assuring me that He will Himself put the words in my mouth, this good Master said to me: 'I still have the rod of justice in My hand, and if they wish to snatch it from Me, let them replace it by the Work of Reparation. As for yourself, be faithful in fulfilling your mission. Look upon it as an honor to have been deputed by Me to manifest My Will. Should you prove unfaithful to My voice, you would expose yourself to feel the strokes of that rod.'

"In order to obey the Divine Master, I most humbly pray you, Reverend Mother, to arrange for me a visit from the Archbishop. In case His Excellency is too occupied, then will he be so kind as to send me his Secretary through whom I could transmit the communications I have been commissioned to deliver to my Bishop."

The Archbishop having been acquainted with this urgent development sent his Secretary, Father Vincent, to the Carmelite Convent, and the following is the conversation which took place there, as Sister Mary of St. Peter herself personally recorded it in writing:

"I am going to give a brief sketch of my debate with the Secretary of the Archbishop, on the subject of the Work of the

Reparation. Our Lord has assisted me as He had promised, for I was neither uneasy nor intimidated, and I spoke with the greatest ease. As nearly as I can give it, the following is the account of our conference:

"THE SECRETARY — 'Sister, I came in the name of His Excellency, to say to you that he has shown your letters to the members of his Council, and they unanimously pronounced against the establishment of the Work you ask. The Archbishop has most carefully examined this affair, he has prayed for guidance, and it is impossible for him to approve it in his official capacity, as there is nothing to attest the validity of your mission.'

"SISTER MARY OF ST. PETER — 'Reverend Sir, I do not pretend to plead with His Excellency anew on this point, or to argue concerning my sentiments in regard to the mission which I believe has been imposed on me by our Lord for the salvation of our country. My intention here has been only to comply with the promptings of my conscience. When I had the honor to speak to His Excellency of the communications I thought I received from God, he answered me thus, "My Child, do not be disturbed, about this being an illusion. It is not so in my opinion, for I recognize here the seal of God." Reverend Sir, it is these words which I received as coming from the Holy Spirit, that have made me persevere in my mission.'

"THE SECRETARY — 'My good Sister, His Excellency said this to you at that time, not knowing how far the matter would go. Since then he has carefully examined it, he has prayed, and he has decided in the negative.'

"SISTER MARY OF ST. PETER — 'This is sufficient for me. I wished only to know His Excellency's decision. My conscience urged me to take these steps towards advancing the establishment of the Work of the Reparation. Now that I have done so I am perfectly at peace. Furthermore, my reason for desiring to speak to the Archbishop was to acquit myself of my mission.

[215]

Therefore, since you are his representative, I now, as an act of religion, lay my mission at the feet of the ecclesiastical authority, with whom will rest the responsibility before God.'

"THE SECRETARY — 'But, my good Sister, the Association of which you speak is already established!'

"SISTER MARY OF ST. PETER — 'Yes, Reverend Sir, but the Church of Tours should be its depository. I asked the Archbishop for this, but since he did not judge proper to establish it, I submitted. What now proves that it is really in conformity to the Will of God is the fact that in spite of all this, it was established, although I had no part in it.'

"THE SECRETARY — 'It has many members here, and has not His Excellency approved a small book of prayers belonging to it?'

"SISTER MARY OF ST. PETER — 'Very true, Reverend Sir, but it is necessary that there be a canonically erected Association at Tours. The Work has need of the cooperation and protection of His Excellency, the Archbishop.'

"THE SECRETARY — 'Sister, I tell you in all confidence that this Work established at Langres is not progressing so favorably, and it has excited the comments of the press.'

"SISTER MARY OF ST. PETER — 'Reverend Sir, I am not at all astonished, for our Lord has told me that the demon would do his utmost to annihilate the Work. Was it not so with the devotion to the Sacred Heart of Jesus, and with the institution of the Feast of the Blessed Sacrament? It is true, the Saviour entrusted such missions to worthier souls than I, yet they were persecuted.'

"THE SECRETARY — 'Sister, all God's works excite contradiction and persecution, for example, the Archconfraternity of the Sacred Heart of Mary. This is indeed a beautiful Work including all, for its object is to convert sinners.'

"SISTER MARY OF ST. PETER — 'Our Lord was aware of its

existence, Reverend Sir, when He asked through me for another Confraternity, and He has made known to me that this first was not sufficient, because to obtain the pardon of one we have offended we must make some reparation. Moreover, our Lord has made me understand that it is the transgression of the First Three Commandments of God especially which have aroused His anger against our country. Therefore, Reverend Sir, since both the secular and ecclesiastical arm have been powerless to prevent these disorders, we must, at least, make reparation to God for them.'

"THE SECRETARY — 'Ah, my good Sister, here is the point in question; you say God demands this but we are not sure of it. You may be mistaken.'

"SISTER MARY OF ST. PETER — 'Reverend Sir, this supposition is not impossible, yet I can scarcely believe that a delusion could have lasted five years, as this has, uninfluenced by any one, since my Superiors in their prudence did not encourage me. They even forbade me to think about it, and were unwilling to take it upon themselves to decide the case. Therefore, the Father Superior has already referred all these matters to the judgment of His Excellency.'

"THE SECRETARY — 'Well, then, my good Sister, be perfectly at peace since you have done your duty in making known these communications to His Excellency. Now, I say to you in his name, think no more of all this, but banish it entirely from your mind.'

"SISTER MARY OF ST. PETER — 'But Reverend Sir, the Archbishop certainly does not forbid me to pray to God for the fulfillment of His designs.'

"THE SECRETARY — 'No, but let there be no further requests to establish the Work of Reparation.'

"SISTER MARY OF ST. PETER — 'Reverend Sir, I beg you to assure the Archbishop of my obedience to his commands.' "

Sister Mary of St. Peter walked away from the parlor after her interview with mixed feelings of triumph and regret. She had cause for both. She had done our Lord's will by launching an offensive drive, to establish the Work of Reparation in her diocese by appealing personally to the highest ecclesiastical authority. She had not been ordered to succeed, but only to make a valiant forward effort, and having achieved this, her mission was accomplished.

At the same time, being flatly refused, losing as it were the opening battle, in so important a cause, she could not refrain from grieving. Our Lord hastened at once to console her.

"Our Saviour made me understand," writes Sister Mary, "that His Work of Reparation will only become the more flourishing in the future, for it will grow the stronger and more vigorous in the midst of storms, and that like a ship refused harbor at one port, it will happily land at another."

Then as if to reassure her in a final and most striking manner about the unbounded efficacy of Devotion to the Holy Face, our Lord now declared to her that nothing is more capable of disarming God's irritated justice than to offer Him the Holy Face because the Sacred Head has taken upon Itself the thorns of our sins, and the Holy Face has set itself as a rock under the strokes of that same justice.

"It has canceled our debts," says Sister Mary of St. Peter, "and It is our security. Therefore, our Saviour has commanded me to keep myself constantly before the throne of His Father offering Him this Divine Face, the object of His delight."

But if the Saviour through these words urged His faithful servant, Sister Mary of St. Peter, to continue, in spite of all obstacles, to practice the Devotion to His adorable Face, He also made it clear that the Reparation was not to remain as her private personal devotion merely, but that it was to be spread far and wide.

"Our Lord told me that He wanted this Devotion to His Holy Face MOST ZEALOUSLY propagated."

This statement was destined to be the Saviour's final and irrevocable decree issued to the virgin of Carmel in regard to the Work of Reparation. Its re-emphasis at this stage of developments is self-evident. When two weeks earlier the Secretary in an interview with Sister Mary of St. Peter told her never again to request the establishment of the Work of Reparation in the Diocese of Tours, this negative attitude might indicate to a certain degree an authoritative halting of the Devotion to the Holy Face unless the Saviour Himself reopened the issue, shedding further light on the subject.

The revelation of March, 1848, therefore, taking place only a few days after the interview with the diocesan representative, was a final restatement of the Sovereign Will of our Saviour regarding the Reparation, which doubtless, ultimately paved the way for the Supreme Pontiff himself to be approached, and in due time to render his unerring approval of it.

This was to be the last such plea by our Lord to Sister Mary of St. Peter, climaxing four and one-half years of repeated communications on this subject. Almost at once other unexpected events began rapidly to shape the destiny of Sister Mary of St. Peter. Less than two weeks after her historic interview with the Secretary who enjoined her in the name of the Archbishop not to ask again for the establishment of the Devotion to the Holy Face in the diocese, Sister Mary of St. Peter received a divine communication of culminating importance to herself. Shining with glory, our Lord appeared to the faithful apostle of His Work of Reparation and said:

"You are near the goal of your earthly pilgrimage. The end of the combat approaches. You will soon behold My Face in Heaven . . ." The date of this revelation announcing her fastly approaching death was March 30, 1848.

Although Sister Mary was until now apparently in fair health, following all the religious exercises prescribed by the Holy Rule, and performing all her duties as Portress Sister, she suddenly developed certain alarming symptoms, and after being examined by a physician, she was found to be mortally ill. Besides suffering from severe pulmonary tuberculosis, she also developed an ulcerated throat which fittingly symbolized her role in life, as that of a victim repairing especially for blasphemies uttered by the tongues of guilty men. For two and a half months she was unable to take any solid food whatever and subsisted only on a small quantity of liquids. Enduring her pains with resignation, and even joy, she prayed almost constantly for the salvation of souls, while she longed to exchange this world for the next.

Shortly before she died she was asked about the Devotion to the Holy Face, to which she answered:

"I have the greatest hopes. The plans of the wicked will be foiled! It was to accomplish this that the Work of Reparation to the Holy Face was revealed. Now that this is done my career is ended for it was for this Work that God had placed me on earth, as our Lord has made known to me. Oh, how true it is that God has means of satisfying His justice which are unknown to men."

Once when she was asked to apply certain of her sufferings for a special intention, she replied:

"I do not know whether I am free to do so because I am entirely consecrated as a victim to the cause of the Work of Reparation."

She died in the odor of sanctity on July 8, 1848, in the thirty-third year of her life, less than four months after the interview she had held with the Secretary who told her that while she was allowed to apply herself personally to the Work of Reparation, she was never again to ask for the establishment of the Work in the diocese. At the time this seemed, indeed, a difficult order to fulfill for one who was by Divine Providence selected as an Apostle to work for the propagation of the Cult of the Holy Face as her particular mission in life.

But she who was ever obedient in the spirit and to the very letter of the law during life was to show herself obedient unto death. It was to become a matter of record that she never again asked for the establishment of the Devotion to the Holy Face in her diocese. Her inflamed, ulcerated throat, parched and aching as if pierced by thorns, allowed for no more verbal addresses, and thus in one stroke of Providence, she was freed forever from the burden of repeating her requests for the establishment of the great Work of Reparation for whose triumph she had offered herself as a victim.

Now, dying as that victim, she would attain her end in the same manner as did her Divine Model, Who offered Himself because it was His Own will, and dying as a holocaust on the cross achieved His goal, the redemption of the human race.

After her death, Reparation through the Devotion to the Holy Face was chiefly kept up through the fervor of a wealthy retired lawyer of Tours, a devoted friend of the deceased nun, Leo Dupont. Having procured a picture of the Holy Face, which was touched to the true relic of the veil of Veronica at the Vatican, this exemplary Christian hung it on a prominent wall of his drawing room before which he ever kept a lamp burning, as a token of veneration.

So many extraordinary favors were granted to those who prayed before this picture that the residence of this lawyer became a private place of pilgrimage. For the next thirty years, that is to the very end of his life, Leo Dupont kept the flame of Reparation alive in his home for the benefit of all who wished to intercede to God before it. Three months after his saintly death, his home was transformed into a public chapel.

Soon afterwards the Work of Reparation was referred to the decision of the Supreme Pontiff, Leo XIII, who wholeheartedly approved the Devotion, through the formality of a Papal Brief.

So was erected in perpetuity the Archconfraternity of Reparation in the Oratory of Leo Dupont, in 1885, where until the present day priests still carry on the mission of Sister Mary of St. Peter, to whom our Lord revealed a hundred years ago the real weapon that is destined for the overthrow of Communism. That weapon is Devotion to the Holy Face as a means of Reparation for the outrageous crimes of modern freethinkers, atheists, blasphemers and the profaners of the Lord's day, which are the evils that more than any other cry to Heaven for vengeance and that today bring us face to face with the threat of an atomic war whose consequence would admittedly be the destruction of all civilization as we know it.

PART IV

PRAYERS OF REPARATION

St. Veronica and the veil on which Our Lord miraculously imprinted the image of His countenance when Veronica presented Him with the veil to wipe His face on His sorrowful journey to Calvary.

THE GOLDEN ARROW

This prayer was dictated by our Lord Himself to Sister Mary of St. Peter. Opening His Heart to her, our Saviour complained of blasphemy, saying that this frightful sin wounds His divine Heart more grievously than all other sins, for it was like a "poisoned arrow."

After that, our Saviour dictated the following prayer, which He called *"The Golden Arrow,"** saying that those who would recite this prayer would pierce Him delightfully, and also heal those other wounds inflicted on Him by the malice of sinners. This prayer is regarded as the very BASIS of the Work of Reparation. It is recommended for recitation on each of the thirty-three beads of the Holy Face Chaplet.

---

*See next page.

PRAYER OF REPARATION
IN PRAISE OF THE
HOLY NAME OF GOD ENTITLED

"THE GOLDEN ARROW"

MAY THE MOST HOLY, MOST SACRED, MOST ADORABLE, MOST INCOMPREHENSIBLE AND UNUTTERABLE NAME OF GOD BE ALWAYS PRAISED, BLESSED, LOVED, ADORED AND GLORIFIED, IN HEAVEN, ON EARTH AND UNDER THE EARTH, BY ALL THE CREATURES OF GOD, AND BY THE SACRED HEART OF OUR LORD JESUS CHRIST, IN THE MOST HOLY SACRAMENT OF THE ALTAR. AMEN.

After receiving this prayer, Sister Mary of St. Peter was given a vision in which she saw the Sacred Heart of Jesus delightfully wounded by this *"Golden Arrow"* as torrents of graces streamed from It for the conversion of sinners.

Offering of the Holy Face of Our Lord Jesus Christ to God the Father in Order to Appease His Justice and Draw Down Mercy Upon Us

Prayer

Eternal Father, turn away Your angry gaze from our guilty people whose face has become unsightly in Your eyes. Look instead upon the Face of Your Beloved Son, for this is the Face of Him in Whom You are well pleased. We now offer You this Holy Face, covered with shame and disfigured by bloody bruises in reparation for the crimes of our age in order to appease Your anger, justly provoked against us. Because Your divine Son, our Redeemer, has taken upon His Head all the sins of His members, that they might be spared, we now beg of You, Eternal Father, to grant us mercy. AMEN.

AN ASPIRATION TO THE ETERNAL FATHER TO BE FREQUENTLY RECITED DURING THE DAY

ETERNAL FATHER, we offer You the Holy Face of Jesus, covered with blood, sweat, dust and spittle, in reparation for the crimes of communists, blasphemers, and for the profaners of the Holy Name and of the Holy Day. AMEN.

PRAYER TO REPRODUCE THE IMAGE OF GOD IN OUR SOULS

Our Lord told Sister Mary of St. Peter that the Image of His Holy Face is like a Divine Stamp which, if applied to souls, through prayer, has the power of imprinting anew within them the Image of God.

PRAYER

I SALUTE YOU, I ADORE YOU, AND I LOVE YOU, OH, ADORABLE FACE OF MY BELOVED JESUS, AS THE NOBLE STAMP OF THE DIVINITY! COMPLETELY SURRENDERING MY SOUL TO YOU, I MOST HUMBLY BEG YOU TO STAMP THIS SEAL UPON US ALL, SO THAT THE IMAGE OF GOD MAY ONCE MORE BE REPRODUCED BY ITS IMPRINT IN OUR SOULS. AMEN.

PRAYER TO OBTAIN
THE SETTLEMENT OF ALL OUR NEEDS

Oh, Eternal Father, since it has pleased our Divine Saviour to reveal to mankind in our present century the power residing in His Holy Face, we now avail ourselves of this Treasure in our great needs. Since our Saviour Himself promised that by offering to You, Oh, Eternal Father, the Holy Face disfigured in the Passion, we can procure the settlement of all the affairs of our household, and that nothing whatsoever will be refused us, we now come before Your Throne.

Offering to You, Oh, God, this adorable Countenance, disfigured with painful bruises and covered with shame and confusion, we beg through the merits of this Holy Face to obtain these, our most pressing needs.

Grant us pardon, Eternal Father, for the worst crimes of our age, which are atheism, blasphemy, and the desecration of Your holy days.

Avert from us destruction by war and its consequences which loom through the malice of revolutionary men who have risen up to stamp out religion from the face of the earth through false indoctrination, and who now stand ready to impose their wicked designs with militaristic force. May this offering of the Holy Face of our Saviour before Your throne of majesty obtain for us deliverance from these evils.

Send us, Oh, God, zealous and enlightened laborers, by conferring many vocations to the priesthood and to religion, so that by their prayers, their works, and their sacrifices they may spread the blessings of Your Church and confound Your enemies. AMEN.

The Holy Face of Jesus
from the Shroud of Turin.

AFTERWORD

The aim of this book is to revive devotion to the Holy Face of Jesus as a means of Reparation to God for the crimes committed against His Divine Majesty. The question may be asked, was not this Devotion of Reparation universally practiced in the Church some years ago? The answer is, yes, it was widespread for many years after the Brief of Pope Leo XIII canonically established the Archconfraternity of the Holy Face in 1885. Unfortunately, however, it was neglected and forgotten in the years immediately prior to the First World War in 1914. Was it not perhaps due to our failure to continue this Reparation, as demanded by Our Divine Lord in His revelations to the holy Carmelite of Tours, that God allowed the "malice of wicked men" to precipitate us into two world conflicts, with all their indescribable horrors?

And now, when we live daily on the verge of a Third World War, which threatens total destruction because of atomic weapons presently in the hands of our enemies, shall we at last embrace this reparation demanded by Our Lord? The "revolutionary men," designated by Our Lord Himself as Communists, have so engulfed the world in turmoil that humanity itself faces destruction. This is the consensus of opinion from all unimpeachable sources, including Pope Pius XII, who warned that there persists a general world condition which "may explode at any moment."

Addressing Himself mystically to the pious Carmelite nun, Our Lord told her that especially to His priests He promises that He will defend them before His Father in Heaven and give them His kingdom if they, through words, prayers or writings, defend His cause in this work of "reparation." Pastors, therefore, and priests who desire to answer this call should endeavor, through regular procedure, to establish the Confraternity of the Holy Face in their parishes.

PROMISES OF OUR LORD JESUS CHRIST IN FAVOR OF THOSE WHO HONOR HIS HOLY FACE

1. All those who honor My Face in a spirit of reparation will by so doing perform the office of the pious Veronica. According to the care they take in making reparation to My Face, disfigured by blasphemers, so will I take care of their souls which have been disfigured by sin. My Face is the seal of the Divinity, which has the virtue of reproducing in souls the image of God.

2. Those who by words, prayers or writing defend My cause in this Work of Reparation I will defend before My Father, and will give them My Kingdom.

3. By offering My Face to My Eternal Father, nothing will be refused, and the conversion of many sinners will be obtained.

4. By My Holy Face, they will work wonders, appease the anger of God and draw down mercy on sinners.

5. As in a kingdom they can procure all that is desired with a coin stamped with the King's effigy, so in the Kingdom of Heaven they will obtain all they desire with the precious coin of My Holy Face.

6. Those who on earth contemplate the wounds of My Face shall in Heaven behold it radiant with glory.

7. They will receive in their souls a bright and constant irradiation of My Divinity, that by their likeness to My Face they shall shine with particular splendor in Heaven.

8. I will defend them, I will preserve them and I assure them of Final Perseverance.

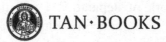